# Action Research for Teacher Candidates

## Using Classroom Data to Enhance Instruction

Edited by Robert P. Pelton

Foreword by Richard Sagor

ROWMAN & LITTLEFIELD EDUCATION
Lanham, Maryland • New York • Toronto • Plymouth, UK
2010

KH

Published in partnership with the Association of Teacher Educators

Published in the United States of America
by Rowman & Littlefield Education
A division of Rowman & Littlefield Publishers, Inc.
A wholly owned subsidary of The Rowman & Littlefield Publishing Group, Inc.
4501 Forbes Boulevard, Suite 200, Lanham, Maryland 20706
http://www.rowmaneducation.com

Estover Road, Plymouth PL6 7PY, United Kingdom

British Library Cataloguing in Publication Information Available

**Library of Congress Cataloging-in-Publication Data**

Action research for teacher candidates / edited by Robert P. Pelton.
    p. cm.
  Includes bibliographical references.
  ISBN 978-1-60709-692-4 (cloth : alk. paper) — ISBN 978-1-60709-693-1 (pbk. :
alk. paper) — ISBN 978-1-60709-694-8 (electronic)
  1. Action research in education. 2. Teachers—In-service training. I. Pelton,
Robert P., 1966–
LB1028.24.B47 2010
370.72—dc22                                                     2010017907

∞™ The paper used in this publication meets the minimum requirements of
American National Standard for Information Sciences—Permanence of Paper
for Printed Library Materials, ANSI/NISO Z39.48-1992.
Manufactured in the United States of America.

10/17/11

# Contents

# Foreword

*Action Research for Teacher Candidates* is more than a valuable addition to teacher-education literature and a valuable resource for the preservice educator; it is an important addition to a movement to remake our nation's schools into true professional learning communities.

In the introductory chapter, Robert Pelton correctly reports that "the earliest advocates of the action research movement recognized the practicing teacher as the most effective person to identify educational issues and develop appropriate solutions." This observation is as true today as it was when action research first entered the schoolhouse. Sadly, for years there were no reasonable mechanisms for teachers to learn about and practice the habits of mind and techniques of educational action research. By helping to make disciplined inquiry a significant part of the induction experience of new teachers, Robert Pelton and his colleagues are taking an important step toward making reflective practice the norm for the teaching and learning environment. One simply cannot overstate the importance of the paradigm shift this represents.

In this book Pelton argues, "It is imperative that educators become lifelong learners who are constantly evolving to provide the best possible education to every student." Furthermore, he points out that when preservice teachers engage in action research, "they report an increased level of self-confidence and enthusiasm. They feel empowered because their role in the school becomes meaningful and broadened." These findings from his observations of preservice teachers underscore a key benefit we will see from the incorporation of action research into the induction and preparation experience of future educators: an empowered and fully engaged professional educator.

The recent high rate of teacher attrition in the public schools of the United States has created numerous tragic consequences. Turnover adversely affects school cohesiveness and program continuity. But, more important, too frequently it is the best and brightest of our new teachers who leave their jobs after just a few years. Why does this happen? The evidence suggests that there are two factors: feelings of professional inadequacy and isolation. The habits and processes outlined in this book address both of these persistent problems.

In the pages of this book, teacher candidates will learn how to collect data that will help their students improve academically and behaviorally, while providing the teacher candidate with credible evidence of their personal professional effectiveness. This is what produces the "self-confidence and enthusiasm" Pelton's own research has documented as a benefit of action research. Furthermore, the encouragement of reflective practice and collegial discourse through action research at the earliest stages of a teacher's career will make it likely that the new generation of teachers will bring a perspective into the schoolhouse that will make professional isolation a thing of the past.

In searching for an accurate descriptor for the modern teacher, I have become attached to the metaphor of educational architect. This metaphor avoids the debate of whether teaching is an art or science and asserts that it is an inextricable mix of both. The architect must bring a mastery of many knowledge bases to their practice, but regardless of how long the architect has practiced, each and every project requires the application of creative problem solving to address the needs of unique settings, contexts, and clients. The same is true of educational architects who encounter new action research challenges with every class they teach. That aspect of teaching, which requires joining craft knowledge with reflection and creative problem solving, presents challenges that will keep teaching gratifying, for the best and brightest of this new generation of teachers, for years to come. Specific strategies and examples on how to accomplish this while improving student performance can be found throughout this book.

While this book was designed primarily for the preservice teacher, I encourage every reader who purchases this book to hold to it and keep it in a prominent place in their professional library. The descriptions of the action research process and examples provided in chapters 1–3 will be worth returning to and reviewing repeatedly throughout one's career.

Ultimately the greatest virtue of an action research approach to professional development is that it can never get stale. There are and will always be new challenges crying out for the creativity of the reflective practitioner. Action research as promoted by Pelton and his colleagues can focus on virtually anything one might encounter as a professional educator. For this reason I encourage every reader to read chapter 4, "Action Research and the Early Childhood Educator," even if they don't teach young children. Likewise, readers should review chapter 7, "Action Research to Change Student Behavior," even if they currently have no issues with classroom management. I say this because these chapters underscore the applicability of the habits and tools of action research for addressing whatever issues or circumstances an educator will ever face. Finally, the discussions of lesson study, teacher work sample methodology, and response to intervention (RtI) merit everyone's consideration. Not only do these chapters provide valuable insights into these promising practices as examples of the action research process but they also introduce modes of professional development with tremendous promise for fostering lifelong professional learning.

It is my hope and dream that the readers of this book will find teaching to be the most rewarding of possible career choices. I hope to see them become leaders in their schools and of their profession. The habits they will learn from the conduct of action research will pay many dividends as they progress through their careers. It is no surprise that to prove one's excellence and qualifications for National Board Certification, the National Board for Professional Teaching Standards has required applicants to engage in precisely the practices this book so effectively promotes.

I am excited to think of the work that will be done by the preservice teachers who use this book. I am even more excited, however, when I think of the thousands of our nation's children who will reap the benefits that will flow from their future years of working with teachers who fully understand, and embrace, reflective practice.

Best wishes to all of you and enjoy the journey.

—Richard "Dick" Sagor, director of The Instititute for the
Study of Inquiry in Education and a major contributor to the
field of classroom-based teacher research

# Preface

I have long believed that teachers themselves will be the ones who transform our nation's schools. For too long, we have been pressed to look elsewhere instead of our own classrooms for answers. Federal mandates and trendy programs have not brought the necessary results we seek.

This book is an acknowledgment that teachers are the single most important element in helping every child succeed in school. This book has been written in the hopes of equipping teachers-in-training—that is, *teacher candidates*—with the skills of action research, a process that leads to focused, effective, and responsive strategies that help students succeed.

## VOICE

Throughout this field-based book, we will speak directly to the teacher-in-training who is in the field and seeks to *learn and do* action research.

## OVERVIEW

Understanding the value and potential of action research will serve you now as you develop your teaching skills and as you progress on your way to becoming a reflective, thoughtful, and effective educator. In years to come, having the mindset and skill sets of an action researcher will serve you well as you become an exemplary teacher. Those of us who have adopted the philosophy and methods of action research have experienced the success of this approach on teaching and learning. The action researchers you will meet within the pages of this book are convinced that you will soon begin to share their enthusiasm for this experiential-based, result-producing process of self-development and pedagogical excellence.

## ABOUT THIS BOOK

The development of this field-based book is a direct result of doing action research. Educators from across practical and pedagogical areas of expertise have come together to reflect upon their own and each other's work in action research. They hold a variety of positions, including college professors, classroom teachers, and some recently graduated interns as well. Each has explored and integrated best practices and wishes to share the results with you. Every chapter has gone through a series of feedback loops and has evolved into a supportive resource that can be used by teachers-in-training as they learn and do action research. The knowledge we have learned is going to be yours! Our hope is that it serves you well.

The information in the pages that follow can be used by college supervisors, school supervisors, and specialists in the schools or by administrators who seek to support teachers and teacher candidates, who are learning about and are doing their own action research. We believe that anyone who is interested in school-based action research will find this text useful and informative. The driving force behind the development of this text is to provide a user-friendly resource so beneficial that it becomes the most valuable tool in your classroom or your book bag, serving you as a reference throughout your entire teaching career.

## HOW IS THIS TEXT ORGANIZED?

Rather than attempting to read this text from cover to cover, begin by skimming the pages. Part I, "Understanding Action Research," gives an overview of the fundamentals of action research, its history, and how it is unfolding and currently being used in classrooms just like yours. Included is a process that can be used to focus on almost any classroom issue that you believe should be addressed. Additionally, you will learn to utilize quantitative and qualitative data when conducting your action research. This section will help ensure that your action research project is well-grounded in the fundamentals of the process

Part II, "A Cross Section of Action Research Applications," provides additional ways to implement action research in the school setting and explores potential areas of interest that you might pursue. You will learn how to apply action research with even the youngest of learners. You will be introduced to the system of *action research-lesson study*, which can be applied across grade levels or in a specific content area. You will learn action research techniques specific to special education and gain knowledge of Response to Intervention (RtI), an action research framework aimed at preventing academic failure through early intervention. You will also see how action research can be used to create and sustain behavioral change. These topics will be covered, plus the popular form of intern-driven action research known as *teacher work sample methodology* will be made available to you!

## WHY DO ACTION RESEARCH?

Every step you take and every discovery you make through action research will enhance your teaching practices. Your mindset and skills as an action researcher will also validate what you might already know about teaching—that *YOU* are the single most important element in helping every child succeed. Now go out and do it!

# I

## UNDERSTANDING ACTION RESEARCH

# 1

# An Introduction to Action Research

*Robert P. Pelton, EdD, Professor of Education, School of Education, Stevenson University, Maryland*

## INTRODUCTION

Action research, in the school setting, is a systematic approach to improve teaching practices. It is a simple process, and if you learn how to use it, it will meet many of your teaching goals. You will find that the methods of action research are designed to answer one of the most basic questions in education: How well are my students learning what I intend to teach? After all, isn't student learning the most important goal of teaching?

Much has been written about the positive effects of using action research in the school environment (Calhoun 2002; Darling-Hammond & Baratz-Snowden 2007; Mills 2007; Pelton 2007; Sagor 2009). In this chapter, you will be introduced to the mindset and skill sets of an action researcher. The remainder of this volume is focused on helping you learn and do action research. You will find that this highly effective model of classroom inquiry, presented in the coming pages, will serve you well now as you learn the art of teaching and in the future as you become an exemplary teacher.

## CHAPTER OBJECTIVES

By the time you finish reading and thinking about this chapter you will be able to:

- Define action research.
- Describe how the *reflection-in-action* mindset serves you as a teacher candidate.
- List the five stages of the action research process.
- Describe the evolution of action research and why it is becoming popular in teacher preparation programs.


## WHAT IS ACTION RESEARCH?

A simple way to understand action research is take a look at the term itself and separate its parts. "Action" means pretty much what you might think it would. In terms of action research, the *action* is what you do as a teaching professional in the classroom. Creating the learning environment, interacting with your students, developing lesson plans, assigning homework, and almost everything you do in your daily routine of teaching constitutes the "action" of action research.

The "research" part of action research refers to the methods, habits, and attitudes you will learn about in this book. The methods of data collection, the professional habits of observation, the attitude of openly searching for new and better ways to present material and challenge your students, and the disposition to be a reflective practitioner will all be covered in the coming pages. Before long, you will develop the ability to reflect upon your actions with intention. Your purposeful reflections will shape your future actions. These are among the many skills you will craft as you proceed with this process.


## THE VALUE AND POTENTIAL OF ACTION RESEARCH

### Becoming an Action Researcher

As mentioned earlier, the methods of action research are designed to answer the most basic question of education: *How well are my students learning what I am teaching?* However, it must be stressed that there *is* something more important than the answer to the original question. The central focus of becoming an action researcher is how you *respond* to the answer to that most basic question. You may have feedback and information on your students' learning, including your personal observations and their test scores, but what are you doing with such data? You may be pondering what your next step should be. If your students are doing well, what can you do to enrich their learning? If they are not doing well, what can you do to improve their learning or test results? Reflection on student learning is what all good teachers do naturally, and it is a skill that can be developed by doing action research.

Action researchers believe that the real solutions for meeting the challenges of educating today's students lie in the expertise of the teacher and how they effectively use the information or "data" that is generated by their students in their classrooms each and every day. Action research is simply an organized, proven, and reliable process for ensuring that you use the data in your classroom to evolve into the high quality educator that your students need and deserve.

You will find that the habits and practices of conducting classroom action research will serve you as you begin your teaching career and in the future as you become a leading teacher. You may experience some apprehension about your ability to implement your first action research project. This is expected and a perfectly normal way to feel. That is the primary reason the authors created this field-based book!

As you become more familiar with the various skills of an action research oriented teacher, you will find that eventually these practices mesh seamlessly with your own daily work as a skilled educator. Action research will become one of your habits of mind for teaching and your modus operandi as a reflective practitioner. It will not be something added on to your normal teaching responsibilities. The action research process is actually quite simple. The authors' experience has shown that, with guidance, you can use this process effectively in a relatively short period of time. This book will support your efforts in action research and guide you through the process so you can successfully proceed in your goal of becoming an effective teacher and reflective practitioner.

### Developing an Action Research Mindset (*Reflection in Action*)

Action research is best seen as a way you approach your work in the classroom and school setting. Think of it as a *mindset* for teaching. It is a powerful mindset for teaching because it emphasizes your role as a reflective practitioner who is continually observant, thoughtful, and willing to examine personal actions in the light of the best possible practices for your students. Becoming an action researcher goes well beyond just doing an action research project; it involves developing a reflection-in-action mindset toward your teaching.

As a teacher candidate, you have spent a great deal of time reflecting on your actions by keeping journals and responding to lesson observations as part of the many different activities you have participated in during your teacher training. As an action researcher, your reflective skills are going to stretch a little further. Instead of reflecting *on* action, you will be developing the skills of reflection *in* action.

A *reflection-in-action* practitioner continuously considers the impact of their actions while they are being implemented, not just after they are implemented or after a marking period concludes. The concept of reflection in action is not entirely new to educational philosophy. The innovative thinking of Donald Alan Schon (1987) brought the notion to us that professional educators need to think about what they are doing *while* they are doing it. In the course of doing action research, you will begin to grasp the importance of reflecting *while* you are teaching as well as throughout the entire action research process.

Although you will start out following a process set forth in this book for doing action research and becoming a reflective practitioner, the more you do it, the more it will become part of who you are as a teacher. It will become your mindset for teaching and you will see that you will apply the reflection-in-action mindset intuitively, assessing your teaching techniques by seamlessly monitoring student learning in a constant cycle of "action-data-reflection," and then continued action, as shown in figure 1.1.

By reflecting in action, you inform your understanding of yourself as a teacher and your children as learners. Your understanding will determine your next actions: the end of one learning experience for you and your students will be the beginning of the next. By adopting a reflection-in-action mindset, your teaching strategies will constantly evolve and improve because you are monitoring your own professional growth and development based upon data generated in your own classroom.

## Improving Student Achievement through Action Research

In truth, your performance as a professional will be measured in part by the scores your students achieve on their standardized tests. Additionally, the determination if schools are succeeding or failing is based on the results of such tests.

Waiting until yearly test results are posted to determine the effectiveness of instructional strategies and student needs is precisely what leaves many children behind. Teachers who are action researchers don't base their teaching decisions solely on such limited data. Action research teachers are constantly evaluating their classroom performance by identifying both the successes and challenges of their students.

As you develop the action research mindset of reflection in action (as discussed above), and the subsequent appropriate modification of teaching practices, you will consistently see positive effects on student achieve-

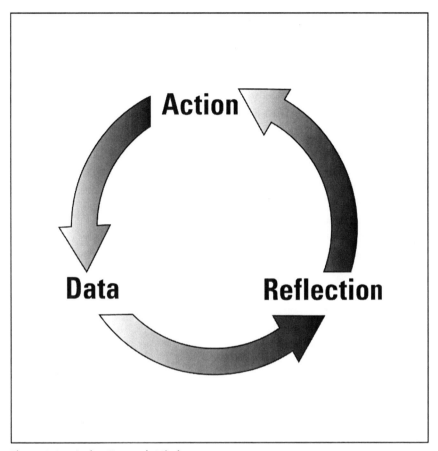

**Figure 1.1.　Action Research Mindset**

ment. This will be a direct result of using the action research processes outlined in this book. The more you use action research and operate from the action research mindset, the more you will see how this proactive style of teaching is self-correcting and that educational decisions should not be exclusively dependent on the results of benchmark exams and high stakes tests.

Action research is a model for teaching with high transparency that enables teachers to determine student achievement on a daily basis rather than waiting for the end of a quarter. Teachers using the reflection-in-action model will have the satisfaction of knowing that students will do well on standardized tests, because appropriate changes have been made throughout the learning process. Such responsive changes are based upon the action researcher's purposefully developed habits of data collection, reflection in action, and self-evaluation, motivated by a deep commitment to implement the most effective teaching strategies available.

## THE ACTION RESEARCH PROCESS

### Getting Started with Action Research

Teachers often use the action research process under many different circumstances and in slightly different ways. That is one of the advantages of the action research model; the process is inherently flexible in order to address the variety of issues that might arise in the teaching and learning environment. However, the fundamentals of the process are the same. That is what we will focus on next.

### The Five Step Action Research Process

Action researchers follow a process such as the one described below to guide their practice:

- Step 1: Issue Identification
- Step 2: Data Collection
- Step 3: Action Planning
- Step 4: Plan Activation
- Step 5: Outcome Assessment

Action researchers are often engaged in a series of "steps"; however, the approach is one that does not always need to proceed in a straight line. You will often find yourself looping back to a previous stage before moving forward to the next. We will examine this more thoroughly later in the chapter, but first let's take a look at how the overall method works by examining the Five Step Action Research Process, as shown in figure 1.2.

Now that you can see the entire action research process, let's have a closer look at each of five action research steps.

#### Step 1: Issue Identification

*Issue identification* starts with you. You may get a hunch or a feeling about something that you would like to investigate. Go for it! Keep a pad and pencil next to your bed. Major breakthroughs and concerns often emerge at odd hours. Write them down.

Perhaps you are questioning some teaching tradition and you think you can improve upon it. That may be your issue. Your teacher intuitions and

**Figure 1.2. The Action Research Process**

hunches are powerful and valued in the action research process. Some of the most influential and best practices can start with a vague feeling about something. Remember, action research is for the benefit of *you* and *your* students.

Action research is often used by teachers to solve problems in their classrooms and schools because it is such an excellent problem-solving process. But do not make the mistake of thinking that you must have some "problem" to solve before undertaking an action research project. By taking an exclusively problem-centered approach, you risk overlooking important opportunities for growth and enhancement. Issue identification is a broader, more inclusive term indicating the limitless scope of possibilities you might choose to investigate.

Of course, you could identify any number of problems you may wish to tackle using the action research process, but you should also be aware of the numerous opportunities you have as an educator to enrich and expand upon in an already successful learning environment.

Exceptional teachers are always looking for ways to push themselves and encourage their children to achieve new levels of learning. Maybe you want to examine the results of using Howard Gardner's Theory of Multiple Intelligences in your classroom teaching. Perhaps you may take on the issue of reducing the literacy gap, or finding a more engaging way to present a certain kind of math lesson. Several teacher candidates in one school initiated an action research project that focused on how they were meeting the needs of students identified as "gifted and talented." The results included changes to the program that further enhanced the students' educational experiences.

To take full advantage of the power and potential of the action research process, get into the positive habit of looking for a variety of issues you may wish to investigate. Sometimes you can jump-start your thinking about an issue to address by using a seed phrase like one of the following:

- Something I would like to improve upon is . . .
- I have a concern about . . .
- I would like to see a change in the way my students . . .
- Something I would like to integrate into my classroom is . . .
- Something I would like to investigate is . . .
- Something I would like to see evolve is . . .

If you are having trouble trying to identify an issue, tap into those around you. Brainstorming with others is a powerful experience and can help you to clarify your issue. Those in your immediate learning environment, including your fellow teachers or teacher candidates, can make excellent partners to help you sort through the issue identification stage of your project. Remember the reflection-in-action mindset? Well, it starts here when you begin your action research. You should plan to have dialogues with others at your school and university to discuss and reflect upon the issue you want to study.

Consider starting out by collaborating with your mentor teacher. Mentor teachers have years of practical experience and love to help others be engaged in authentic learning. If you know of others who are doing or have done action research, seek them out. Action researchers are collaborative by nature and enjoy helping each other. They embrace a culture of inquiry and will support your work.

You will find chapter 3, "Developing an Action Research Project," extremely helpful as you begin and move through your own action research. Chapters 4–7 also provide further ideas regarding the many unique issues you can explore through action research, such as working with early childhood learners, Lesson Study, response to intervention (RtI), teacher work sample methodology (TWSM), and focusing on behavioral learning needs.

## Step 2: Data Collection

Data is an essential part of action research. Collecting, organizing, and reflecting on your data begin in the initial stages of your action research and is continued through the entire process. Your data can serve to guide and validate current actions, as well as assess the final outcomes of your work.

Developing the habits of mind of an action researcher will make you keenly aware of the wealth of data available in your classroom. Typical classroom data includes student work samples, quizzes, homework, running records, checklists, benchmark tests, standardized test results, a question-and-answer session, the results of an every pupil response, the monitoring of student on-task behaviors, attendance records and children's profiles, and your general observations of student learning.

Paying attention to a range of data provides you with multiple points of view on your classroom, which leads to greater accuracy in planning for a change or enhancement in your teaching practices. Your classroom data must guide your work as an action researcher.

Chapter 2 of this book is dedicated to helping you understand your data. In a short time you will become skilled at collecting, organizing, and reflecting on your data and, most important, responding to it appropriately. Learning these strategies will not only serve you now but also throughout your entire career, as you become an action research oriented educator.

## Step 3: Action Planning

At this stage of your action research, you will create a plan that addresses the issue you identified in step 1. When planning your action, you should reflect upon the issue by exploring it in terms of expert input. Think about all the resources you have available to you when develop your action plan: teachers, specialists, teacher candidates, college or university professors and clinical supervisors, school administrators, professional literature, and this text are all resources.

Step 3 is where the culture of collaboration in action research becomes especially important. Expert teachers generally enjoy sharing their knowledge of teaching and learning, but it is really up to you to tap into them. Contact your local college or university professors and ask them about theories and strategies related to your topic. If you are addressing an issue in math or reading, for example, be sure to access your school specialists; these teachers represent a wealth of knowledge and can often direct you to resources and materials relating to your issue. Contact the professor who taught your methods courses.

Go to these professionals with your current issue, initial data in hand, and discuss what might work best to address your specific students' needs. Access them! Learn from their examples and borrow from their conventional knowledge. However, be cautious not to just copy what someone else has done or do what someone else tells you to do because you may lose the transformative power of the reflection-in-action part of the action research process. Instead, develop *your own* action plan by gleaning information from all your resources. A synthesis of this information will help you to begin identifying and shaping your own best practices.

When planning your action, in addition to the expert counsel available from those in your teaching environment, make use of the collected wisdom of the academic community found in libraries and computer databases. A "review of the literature," described for you in chapter 3, is also part of the discipline of being an action researcher. You will find a growing number of articles published for teachers by teachers. It will be enriching to discover what others have done regarding issues similar to yours.

Librarians generally take a keen interest in students researching topics for practical application and can help you make your search more efficient. Formal databases such as ERIC will help you zero in on those educators working on issues similar to yours. Even Internet surfing can turn up a surprising amount of useful material.

Professional organizations can provide a tremendous amount of information. There is at least one specialized organization for every imaginable area of education. Use all of your resources to gain knowledge about all the possibilities and then consider how to put these ideas into action for your specific area of research interest.

After reviewing the data you have collected, researching the relevant professional literature, and talking with your colleagues, professors, and others in your educational environment, you will now be ready to craft an effective plan of action that addresses the issue you identified in step 1.

*Step 4: Plan Activation*

Now is the moment for which you have prepared! You can begin your action with the knowledge that you have reviewed data, researched best practices, and developed the best possible plan to meet your students' needs. No one can anticipate all of the circumstances that might arise within the daily demands of teaching, so move forward with the confidence that you have developed the best possible plans.

Action research is a dynamic process that allows for last minute fine-tuning and spur of the moment responsive changes as you teach. The goal is to continuously create better results for your students. It is wholly encouraged that, based on data generated by your students, you question the effectiveness of what you are doing early in your research.

Dialoguing with your classroom teacher or referring back to the literature might help you modify or tweak your action research plan. Reflect upon where you are and what you need and ask for assistance when required. Embrace the reflection-in-action mindset we have discussed, keep moving forward, and make changes accordingly. After all, the enterprise of learning about teaching while teaching is a core value of action research.

*Step 5: Outcome Assessment*

At this point in your action research you should begin to put everything you have experienced into perspective by now reflecting upon the outcomes of the actions you took in pursuit of excellence as an educator. You have the original data sets from step 1, and you have new data generated as a result of your actions. You have diverse experiences, observations, and anecdotal records.

Now, what do you do with all of this information: subjective, objective, quantitative, and qualitative? First, analyze your data to determine what impact your actions had on children. This might be a cognitive improvement, an affective change, or even a physical or psychomotor improvement.

You might find that your actions have led to improved children skill sets, classroom behaviors, or some other function in the learning environment. You will use your data to make some inferences. Inferences are the conclusions you draw based on what the data is telling you. Use the data analysis strategies in chapter 2 to help you illustrate your data and assess student impact.

Next, engage with your growing community of action researchers and others in your learning environment to reflect on your experiences. Pinpoint how the process has affected your learning as a teacher-in-training. One of the most important personal outcomes of action research is that you will develop new practical knowledge. Practical knowledge is the expertise and skills you acquire as a result of your own experiences. This is consistent with experiential and cognitive development approaches to learning and education.

The data will help you differentiate what worked and what did not work in your classroom. At this point, you should begin to consider:

- What have you learned about your instructional strategies?
- Will you continue with what you are doing, alter it in some way, or discontinue something you tried in the classroom?

If you were disappointed with any of your expected outcomes, look upon the results as an opportunity for learning and change. You might have uncovered a new problem to be solved, but, as previously suggested, develop the habit of reframing "problems to be solved" into "issues to be investigated." Make this an opportunity to continue your work with the mindset and skill sets of an action research teacher.

Some reflective statements at this point might be as follows:

- Something I learned as a result of my action research is . . .
- One thing I intend to do with this information is . . .
- One thing that worked well was . . .
- Something that didn't work out so well was . . .
- Something I would do differently in the future is . . .
- A change I would make in my approach is . . .
- Someone I think could help me at this point is . . .
- A resource I intend to tap for future work in this area is . . .

Throughout the process of doing action research you will generate ideas and develop new knowledge. In step 5, you pause to consider the implications for this new knowledge. With knowledge comes responsibility. It is reasonable at this point to ask yourself how you will put this new knowledge to use in a broader context. Certainly, you should use your new knowledge to re-inform your teaching. You might use it in your first classroom.

For the reason that you are evolving as a professional in the collaborative world of action researchers, consider sharing your research findings with your principal and colleagues on the faculty where you teach. Teacher candidates report that their action research projects become even richer and more meaningful when the process and results are shared with colleagues (Carboni, Wynn, & McGuire 2007). Some novice action researchers are sometimes able to share their research findings at local, state, or even national education conferences. A few may even be published in recognized education journals.

From the five steps of issue identification, data collection, action planning, plan activation, and outcome assessment, you are developing a mindset of reflection in action while you begin to understand the power and potential of action research for you and your own students. Congratulations!

## The Innate Flexibility of Action Research

As already mentioned, action research is inherently flexible. While doing your action research, you will often loop back to a previous step before moving forward to the next step. Take another look at the Five Step Action Research Process described in figure 1.2 and then consider how the following demonstrates the innate flexibility of the process:

In step 3, Action Planning, you may find yourself at the threshold of a plan of action. You will soon be making choices and engaging in activities that will address the issue you previously identified in step 1. You have collected data and begin to sort through it. You are reflecting upon its possible meanings for your project.

The data has begun to tell you a story about your students. In that stack of papers are clues to answer the next big question: What do I do next? You might think ahead to step 4, Plan Activation. Your next thought may very well be "I need more information, more data." Excellent!

No one expects you to gather your research data and instantly know what to do in the classroom. That is why step 3 is called *Action Planning*. During your action planning, you will continually inventory your resources and practices to ensure that you make your best attempt at utilizing the most beneficial strategies.

Perhaps at this point you may decide to circle back to step 2 and collect more data. Or, maybe your next step is to remember the basic framework of action research. Don't worry, you are not alone. Continue to use your resources and data, and then use your reflection-in-action mindset to help guide your action plan.

You will discover that the *action-data-reflection-action* sequence of action research, as previously shown in figure 1.1, cycles and recycles as you proceed within the larger Five Step Action Research Process (figure 1.2). Action researchers embrace this flexibility because we realize that there is some unpredictability in teaching. We make allowances for the unexpected experiences every educator faces. As you make changes to your research plan, simply document those changes and then continue the process.

### Becoming a Responsive Teacher though Action Research

Now that you are familiar with the action research process, let's consider how the reflection-in-action mindset can really strengthen your day-to-day instructional abilities. When you implement the action research process, positive changes will occur in your classroom over the course of days, weeks, months, and into the years. However, bringing effective change to your class can also be an immediate process *while* you are teaching.

A microcosmic perspective of the action research mindset is to be aware of how your learners are responding to your immediate instruction and then take action based upon their needs in the "here and now." This is called responsive teaching.

Responsive teaching is about applying the reflection-in-action mindset moment to moment, differentiating instruction at the appropriate instant, based on the data that flow from the teaching and learning environment. Practicing responsive teaching builds what is probably the most important professional teaching capacity you can have, that is, to be able to "think on your feet" and respond efficiently and effectively *in the moment.*

As you take action during these "teachable moments," new data will result, affirming the effectiveness of your responsive teaching. At these particular times you are learning about teaching *while* you are teaching, which can only occur in the field, when working with students.

Perhaps at first, even making small changes to your teacher plans will be done cautiously. That is fine. With practice, it will become second nature. Eventually you will get very comfortable adjusting your plans based on what the current data are telling you. The key is to keep on moving forward, take the next step, reflect upon where you are and what you need to do, and respond to the data as they emerge from your teaching and leaning environment. The final outcome will be exemplary teaching and high levels of student learning.

It is inevitable that your best teaching will result from being a responsive teacher. You will become efficient at meeting your students' immediate needs and effective in any environment in which you teach. Responsive teaching is a positive and productive habit of exemplary teachers; it is a skill set that can be developed by doing action research.

## Ensuring a Successful Action Research Project

Before we continue, a word of caution is in order. Not all educators know and understand what action research entails, or even the steps involved. Be sensitive to the fact that action research is relatively new and some educators may be unfamiliar with this approach.

Remember, the action research model emphasizes the concept of mutual collaboration. On the one hand, the educational community has a responsibility to provide you with multiple resources to utilize in the process. On the other hand, you have a responsibility to the educational community, and that means communicating how you are conducting your action research.

As you move through the process, you will potentially be affecting many stakeholders, such as your students, other teachers, administrators, counselors, specialists, and parents. This broader community should be taken into consideration or you may face unnecessary frustration. As you proceed in your own action research, inform your colleagues about the approach and theory provided in this book.

# THE EVOLUTION OF ACTION RESEARCH

As a developing action researcher, you might have be wondering exactly how this method of reflective practice got started, what affect the current school-based applications are having, and future potential of the process. The following should give you a sense of the development of action research and why it continues to grow as excellent strategy for teaching and learning.

## A Theory for Reflective Practice

Much of the conceptual framework and the organizing principles and methods of action research can be identified in progressive educational and social movements from the previous century. You might already be recognizing John Dewey's influence on action research. After all, action research *is* experiential learning, and action researchers easily recognize the wisdom and possibilities inherent in this, just as Dewey and other constructivist theorists did.

In his 1938 classic book for educators, *Experience and Education*, Dewey focused primarily on the power of experiential learning. Dewey wrote extensively about the process of reflection and action, by introducing his readers to the relationship between experience and learning. Dewey stressed that experience leads to learning and learning informs the way we approach new experiences. What Dewey could not have foreseen is the way in which experiential leaning has become the focus of teacher education under the term *action research*.

Although the term *action research* had not been coined, Dewey would certainly recognize and applaud the contemporary educators' application of this form of experiential learning in pursuit of pedagogical excellence. Dewey did, however, go as far as to propose that teachers should reflect upon their work as educators and investigate school-based problems through disciplined inquiry (Bednarz 2002).

Consider for a moment other contributions to the foundation of action research such as that of the great Swiss theorist Jean Piaget, who noted the cyclical process of cognitive development in which new knowledge is constructed on the basis of experience and reflection. Piaget observed that learning is a process, which he called *schema development*. Piaget asserted that by assimilating knowledge from previous experiences (actions) and then making mental accommodations (reflection), an adaptation or "learning" has occurred. His explanation of cognitive development certainly validates the action research mindset.

Another substantiation of action research as a justifiable theory for teaching and learning can be obtained from the work of twentieth-century

Russian developmental psychologist Lev Vygotsky. Vygotsky, like Dewey, emphasized the role of experiential learning. Vygotsky described what he called the student's zone of proximal development (ZPD): under adult guidance, or in collaboration with more capable peers, we can help a child move from what he or she already knows and can do, to new understandings. Vygotsky asserted that a child's experience (action), when successfully scaffolded (such as in guided reflections), leads to new learning.

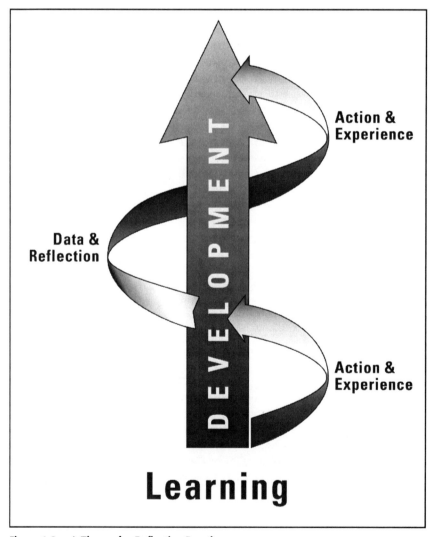

**Figure 1.3.   A Theory for Reflective Practice**

It is clear that the most highly regarded constructivist theorists would agree that knowledge developmental or "learning" is based on a theory of reflective practice; one's experiences build on or are constructed from past experiences and emerge from a continuous process that includes those *actions and experiences*, and the resulting *data and reflection* (guided or independent), which then evolve into new *actions and experiences*, as shown in figure 1.3.

## A Historical Context for Action Research

The person most often recognized as the originator of the modern action research movement is Kurt Lewin. In the early 1940s, Lewin was a prominent researcher and advocate of experimentation with group dynamics in social psychology and human relations training. He founded the Research Center for Group Dynamics at MIT in 1944, where he continued to develop and lay the foundation for what he termed *action research.*

Lewin was the first to conceive action research as a cyclical process consisting of planning, fact finding, action taking, evaluating, and reflecting, followed by more planning, fact finding, and revising (1948). This cyclical process was conducted in a spirit of open inquiry and with the collaboration of all participants. Lewin emphasized the importance of feedback in human communication and established norms for giving and receiving it. His influence extended to the fields of social science, psychology, social psychology, organizational development, process management, change management, and education.

Although clearly influenced by Dewey and deliberately named and shaped by Lewin, it was Stephen Corey, a professor at Teachers College of Columbia University, who brought the terminology and methods of action research to the educational community in the mid-twentieth century.

Barely two years after Lewin's death in 1947, Corey was advocating action research as a process that would facilitate teachers' study of their own practices for the purpose of amending and improving their pedagogical skills. His ideas and methods were subsequently presented in the publication of his 1953 text, *Action Research to Improve School Practices.* In his work, Corey puts forth a specific action research process to be used by "school people" that "gives promise to improving education" (p. 25). The earliest advocates of the action research movement recognized the practicing teacher as the most effective person to identify educational issues and develop appropriate solutions. These research pioneers were talking about you!

Action research fell out of favor in the late 1950s, partly because traditional positivist researchers were skeptical of an approach to acquiring knowledge in which the researcher is involved in the action or process under investigation. The collaborative nature and freeing aspects of action research did not appeal to researchers who were more comfortable working in isolation or to administrators who favored tight control in a top-down approach to organizational structure.

Treating the classroom teacher as an agent of change in the educational hierarchy was not on the traditional researcher's agenda. Furthermore, government-funding sources in the post–World War II era tended to favor the positivist version of educational research emphasizing a detached, objective observer gathering quantitative data and using computer analysis (Baskerville 1999).

What was troubling to the traditional researcher is now one of the great strengths of action research as a method of inquiry. By design, action research *requires* a researcher who is directly involved in the processes and actions being researched. The benefits of training teachers to develop the action research habits of mind and skill sets (habits of observation, information gathering, reflection, collaboration, taking action, and problem solving) was becoming increasingly clear to professional educators and education researchers.

The power of the action research process led to a resurgence of interest within the educational community by the 1970s, most notably in the work of Lawrence Stenhouse, a British researcher who advocated enabling teachers to become active in researching their own practices. In his 1975 text, *An Introduction to Curriculum Research and Development,* he devotes a chapter to this idea under the title "The Teacher as Researcher." In this work Stenhouse advocated "the commitment to systematic questioning of one's own teaching as a basis for development; the commitment and the skills to study one's own teaching; the concern emphasized was to question and test theory in practice by the use of those skills" (p. 144). Thus the *teacher-as-researcher* branch of the action research movement was born.

### Action Research in the Preparation of New Teachers

The rise in popularity of action research is beginning to stir up a worldwide movement in teacher training. In addition to the United States, effective use of action research in teacher preparation programs has been noted in numerous countries, including the United Kingdom, Norway, Finland, Sweden, New Zealand, Germany, Australia, Turkey, China, Taiwan, and Cambodia (Atay 2007; Cardno 2006; Harrison, Lawson, & Wortley 2005; Lloyd 2002; Ponte, Beijaard, & Wubbels 2004; Smith & Sela 2005). In the United States, interest in action research continues to build as its value is documented and recognized by researchers, teachers, and administrators.

One of the most well-know experts in action research, Dr. Marilyn Cochran-Smith, Director of Doctoral Programs in Curriculum and Instruction at Boston College, advocates action research as one of the most direct paths to accountability in teacher training (2004). Dr. Cochran-Smith emphasizes that teacher candidates should be trained to learn from their own practice by analyzing teaching and learning events, thus recognizing which student needs are being met and which are not. She insists that candidates should be able to demonstrate the connections between teacher learning, professional practice, and student learning (2006), all of which can be accomplished through action research.

Action research belongs in teacher-training programs, because it is an ideal curriculum fit for preparing teachers in our schools of education. It is now clearer than ever that beginning teachers need consistent opportunities to apply what they are learning, to analyze what happens, and to adjust their efforts accordingly.

Preparing teachers to learn from their teaching throughout their careers should start at the beginning of teacher training so that a set of tools are acquired that develop the skills and practices of systematic, purposeful critical inquiry (Darling-Hammond & Friedlander 2008). It is imperative that educators become lifelong learners who are constantly evolving to provide the best possible education to every student. That is the essence of the action research process.

It is logical that action research in teacher preparation programs will continue to grow as it has proven to have a positive effect on teaching skills, as well as a personal effect in impacting teacher dispositions. Teacher candidates who do action research report an increased level of self-confidence and enthusiasm. They feel empowered because their role in the school becomes meaningful and broadened (Bednarz 2002; Carboni, Wynn, & McGuire 2007; Pelton 2007; Price & Valli 2005; Zainuddin & Moore 2004). In a study of action research as a tool to facilitate reflective practice, teacher candidates used such phrases as "The time that I spent observing and gathering data enabled me to better understand not only the student I was observing, but also the classroom where the student was situated" (Carboni, Wynn, & McGuire 2007, p. 57).

In another study on the impact of action research on changes in teaching dispositions, teacher candidates reported in their reflection journals, "All of us in this professional development school now not only understand, intellectually, theories and strategies, we can apply them so that students are really learning." And, "It is amazing when I really see him [the student] learn as a result of the specific things I do with him. He [my student] is starting to really understand what he reads" (Pelton 2007, p. 226). As you can see, action research had a positive effect on these teacher candidates and can have a powerful effect on your own professional growth and development. Action research closes the gap between theory and practice and moves teacher candidates from a position of "performing" lessons to placing a focus on student performance and data-based decision making.

When teacher candidates conduct action research, in-service teachers, administrators, and parents all note the positive role the candidates play in the school setting during their internships. Action research thus is becoming recognized as a key component in developing high quality teachers. School supervisors who have mentored teacher candidates while they are doing action research report:

- teacher candidates build teaching competencies by implementing action research with children;
- action research is an appropriate use of teacher candidates' time; and
- teacher candidates should conduct action research in multiple areas of instruction (Pelton 2007).

The escalation in the use of action research in the preparation of new teachers is clearly on the rise. In a study of 245 American Association of Colleges for Teacher Education (AACTE) institutions documents that nearly half (46.8 percent) of responding institutions included action research projects as a requirement in their teacher candidate programs (Henderson, Hunt, & Wester 1999). Reports from this study cited numerous benefits generated by programs whose candidates do action research, such as increased collaboration, improved relationship between higher education and P–12 schools, improvements in reading, science, and math teaching methods, and the development of integrative approaches in elementary education curriculum. Also noted were improvements in field supervision, the creation of a team-teaching approach, and positive collaborative and professional dispositions within groups of P–12 teachers. All this as a result of action research!

Teachers who are training to teach in Special Education also see many positive outcomes of doing action research. In a study designed to evaluate the use of action research as a tool for developing critical reflection, Lloyd (2002) found that candidates report that doing action research:

- made them feel empowered to take responsibility for their own practice;
- changed their attitudes about research;
- provided a practical methodology that empowered them to make change;
- provided them structure to critically evaluate their practice;
- made them more confident to collaborate; and
- helped them to feel more professional as a result of doing this work.

## ACTION RESEARCH: GO OUT AND DO IT!

As a teacher candidate, you are at a period in your professional development when you are in training. It is evident that you have a depth of commitment to your learning, and you are to be commended for this! Surely you want to be the best teacher that you can possibly become. You are ripe for understanding, and having gotten this far in your teacher preparation program, you clearly have the intellect, skills, and determination to grow and learn.

It is now time for you to move forward and use action research to be a self-evaluative practitioner, capable of making adjustments in your teaching to meet student needs. Keen insight into teaching occurs as a result of action research. It has been demonstrated that lesson planning, classroom management, and differentiated instruction are keys to successful teaching. However, there is no single element more awe inspiring than noting your own direct impact on student achievement.

As your first action research project evolves, you should be encouraged to know that the habits of mind and skills you are developing will serve you well throughout your career. Chapter 3, "Developing an Action Research Project," will get you started on this. As you implement the process, remember that action research not only impacts children, it also impacts you! It is not just another assignment on your way to graduation.

The work you put into developing your expertise as a reflective practitioner and action researcher will help make you a responsive teacher and place you on the forefront of a national movement of educational reform and change. As you proceed from being a teacher-in-training to becoming an exemplary practitioner who utilizes the action research approach, you will do so with the full knowledge that you are not only highly qualified to teach but also a high quality teacher who is also highly desirable to employ!

## QUESTIONS FOR REVIEW AND REFLECTION

1. Identify the Five Step Action Research Process and explain how the innate flexibility of the approach can affect how you might go about implementing the process.
2. How might you and your students benefit by you using a reflection-in-action mindset as you teach?
3. What is responsive teaching?
4. How do historical contexts, educational theory, and current trends support the underpinnings for today's classroom-based action research?
5. Describe what it's like to be an action research teacher.

# REFERENCES

Atay, D. (2007, July). Beginning teacher efficacy and the practicum in an EFL content. *Teacher Development, 11*(2), 203–19.

Baskerville, R. (1999). Investigating information systems with action research. *Communications of the Association for Information Systems, 19*(2). Retrieved from http://cis.gsu.edu/~rbaskerv/CAIS_2_19/index.html.

Bednarz, S. (2002, May). Using action research to implement the national geography standards: Teachers as researchers. *Journal of Geography, 101*(3), 103–11.

Calhoun, E. F. (1993, October). Action research: Three approaches. *Educational Leadership, 51*(2), 62–65.

Calhoun, E. F. (2002, March). Action research for school improvement. *Educational Leadership, 59*(6), 18–24.

Calhoun, E. F. (2004). *Using data to assess your reading program.* Alexandria, VA: ASCD.

Carboni, L., Wynn, S., & McGuire, C. (2007, January). Action research with undergraduate preservice teachers: Emerging/merging voices. *Action in Teacher Education, 29*(3), 50–59.

Cardno, C. (2006, November). Leading change from within: Action research to strengthen curriculum leadership in a primary school. *School Leadership & Management, 26*(5), 453–71.

Cochran-Smith, M. (2004, November). Defining the outcomes of teacher education: What's social justice got to do with it? *Asia Pacific Journal of Teacher Education, 32*(3), 193–212.

Cochran-Smith, M. (2006, March). Ten promising trends (and three big worries). *Educational Leadership, 63*(6), 20–25.

Corey, S. M. (1953). *Action research to improve school practices.* New York: Teachers College Columbia University.

Darling-Hammond, L. (2008, June). A future worthy of teaching for America. *Phi Delta Kappan, 8*(10), 730–36.

Darling Hammond, L., & Baratz-Snowden, J. (Eds.). (2007). A good teacher in every classroom: Preparing the highly qualified teachers our children deserve. *Educational Horizons,* Winter, 111–32.

Darling-Hammond, L., & Friedlander, D. (2008, May). Creating excellent and equitable schools. *Educational Leadership, 65*(8), 14–21.

Dewey, J. (1938). *Experience and education.* New York: Touchstone.

Harrison, J., Lawson, T., & Wortley, A. (2005, October). Facilitating the professional learning of new teachers through critical reflection on practice during mentoring meetings. *European Journal of Teacher Education, 28*(3), 267–92.

Henderson, M., Hunt, S., & Wester, C. (1999, December/January). Action research: A survey of AACTE-member Institutions. *Education, 119*(4), 663–67.

Lewin, K. (1948). *Resolving social conflicts: Selected papers on group dynamics.* New York: Harper & Brothers.

Lloyd, C. (2002). Developing and changing practice in special educational needs through critically reflective action research: A case study. *European Journal of Special Needs Educational, 17*(2), 109–27.

Mills, G. E. (2007). *Action research: A guide for teacher researcher* (3rd ed.). Upper Saddle River, NJ: Pearson.

Pelton, R. P. (2007). From performing to performance: Can the repositioning of teacher candidates create a measurable impact on children's achievement while developing positive teaching dispositions? In T. Townsend & R. Bates (Eds.), *Handbook of teacher education* (pp. 219–28). Netherlands: Springer.

Ponte, P., Ax, J., Beijaard, D., & Wubbels, T. (2004, August). Teachers' development of professional knowledge through action research and the facilitation of this by teacher educators. *Teacher and Teacher Education, 20*(6), 571–88.

Price, J., & Valli, L. (2005, January). Preservice teachers becoming agents of change: Pedagogical implications for action research. *Journal of Teacher Education, 56*(1), 57–72.

Sagor, R. (2000). *Guiding school improvement with action research*. Alexandria, VA: ASCD.

Sagor, R. (2005). *The action research guide book: A four-step process for educators and school teams*. Thousand Oaks, CA: Corwin Press.

Sagor, R. (2009, January). Collaborative action research and school improvement. *Journal of Curriculum and Instruction, 3*(1), 7–14.

Schon, D. A. (1987). *Educating the reflective practitioner*. San Francisco: Jossey-Bass.

Smith, K., & Sela, O. (2005, October). Action research as a bridge between pre-service teacher education and in-service professional development for students and teacher educators. *Journal of European Teacher Education, 28*(3), 293–310.

Stenhouse, L. (1975). *An introduction to curriculum research and development*. London: Heinemann.

Zainuddin, H., & Moore, R. (2004, June). Engaging preservice teachers in action research to enhance awareness of second language learning and teaching. *Teacher Education and Practice, 17*(3), 311–27.

# 2

# Understanding Your Data

*Reagan Curtis, PhD, Associate Professor of Educational Psychology, Department of Technology, Learning and Culture, West Virginia University*

*Jaci Webb-Dempsey, PhD, Associate Professor of Education, School of Education, Fairmont State University, West Virginia*

*Neal Shambaugh, PhD, Associate Professor of Educational Psychology, Department of Technology, Learning and Culture, West Virginia University*

## INTRODUCTION

Engaging in action research leads you, the teacher candidate, to reflect on a variety of sources of information as you strive to understand links between your teaching practice and student learning. You need to understand what constitutes "data" as you design your action research. You need to reflect on your data as it is being collected so that you can make day-to-day teaching decisions that best support your students' learning.

Once you have collected data, there are a variety of strategies for structuring and reflecting on different kinds of data. Using appropriate strategies for the data you collect will eventually lead you to understanding your data so that you can make informed data-based decisions about your teaching practice to increase student learning.

## CHAPTER OBJECTIVES

By the time you finish reading and thinking about this chapter you will be able to:

- Recognize that understanding data influences the entire time span of an action research study from planning to sharing findings.
- Identify multiple quantitative and qualitative data sources that will inform your guiding questions and be feasible to collect while teaching full time.
- Focus interim analyses on your data as you collect it to inform both your research and your teaching decisions on a day-to-day basis.
- Focus in-depth analyses on both group and individual student–level data, once data collection is complete.
- Recognize the importance of looking for consistency across data sources.

## USING DATA

Understanding your data comes through systematic cyclical *reflection in action* across the entire timeline of your action research. The nature of this reflection shifts across time and is aided by specific strategies appropriate to different types of data.

In chapter 1, you were presented with a set of procedures that action researchers generally follow as they engage in classroom-based inquiry. You also learned that the process doesn't always proceed lineally from one step to another, but rather the "observation, reflection, revise, collect new data" sequence of action research cycles and recycles as you proceed. For this reason, you will be using data at many stages of your research.

The way you go about using data will vary from study to study. To keep things simple for our discussion, we will look at data in three very basic stages: (1) before your project begins, (2) as your project unfolds, and (3) after you've finished collecting data (see figure 2.1). These general stages will account for any time you might work with data throughout your entire inquiry study.

How you should think about and use data in each of these stages is different. At first, you should be focused on designing your project and selecting relevant data sources. Your thinking about data sources at this point will be the foundation for subsequent stages. As your project unfolds, it will be important to reflect on what your data show to help you fine-tune your teaching and your research on a day-to-day basis.

Once your data collection wraps up, a more systematic and focused look at your data will help you recognize things you might have missed before.

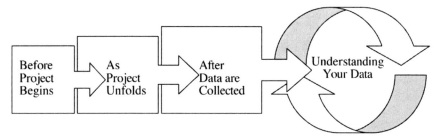

**Figure 2.1. Understanding Data at Each Stage in Action Research**

This final stage is also when you figure out what is most interesting to share with others and how to show your data in ways that help others understand what you have learned.

## UNDERSTANDING DATA BEFORE YOUR PROJECT BEGINS

At this stage, it is important to understand the variety of types of data that can be collected. Everything is potentially data! *If it is information related to your teaching practice, your students' learning, or anything that might impact that learning, then it is potentially meaningful data.* It remains only potentially data, though, until you collect it. That is, until you capture that information in some way so that you can reflect on it, it does not factor into your action research as something that can help you understand how your teaching impacts your learners.

It is important to remember that you cannot capture everything and trying to do too much will make both your teaching and your action research less effective. So, in the early stages, it is important to understand data well enough to select meaningful data sources that will also be feasible for you to capture and reflect upon as you are teaching.

A distinction is commonly made between types of data, that is, qualitative and quantitative. Distinguishing data between these categories is a useful way of beginning to organize your thinking about data sources you might use. With that in mind, we'll first describe several qualitative types of data and then talk about varying types of quantitative data.

As we begin this discussion, you should be thinking about how each of these data sources might help you understand your teaching and your students' learning, without worrying about how to analyze the data in detail . . . we'll get to that later. We'll end this section with a discussion of how qualitative and quantitative types of information can fit together to help you really understand links between your teaching and your students' learning.

## POTENTIAL QUALITATIVE DATA SOURCES

At the most basic level, qualitative data sources are those that are not easily captured with numbers. This is again an oversimplification, but your understanding of the differences between qualitative and quantitative data will strengthen as you continue reading and thinking about this chapter and your action research.

Most often, qualitative data sources are captured through narrative description of what students and teachers do and say. Images (videos, photographs, and artwork), physical objects, and audio recordings are also potential qualitative data sources. These data sources often provide rich descriptive and contextual information about the people, actions, and interactions that occur in classrooms.

Let's examine several of the most common types of qualitative data that can be captured, understanding that this is not meant to be a complete list. As you read about these, remember that data sources in action research should be natural complements to your teaching; they should not be artificial add-ons done only for research purposes that interfere with your teaching practice.

### Student Work Samples, Student Documents

Student work is one of the richest sources of qualitative data. Any assignment or activity that involves a student creating a document becomes a potential data source. We use the term *document* here in a very general sense; a document is any work product.[1]

Often documents are paper with words and numbers on it, but work products such as pictures drawn by students to illustrate stories they have written, volcanoes made out of clay, solar systems made out of Styrofoam and wire, PowerPoint presentations of group research projects, and a multitude of other things students create are equally rich potential sources of qualitative data.

What all of these things have in common is that they are created by students in response to an activity or assignment you gave them. They are examples of how students interpreted what they thought their teacher wanted them to do. They are reflections of student learning given narrative and physical form.

One of the great things about student work samples and documents is that you will ask your students to create them regardless of whether or not you are doing action research. They are a natural part of teaching and learning, and capturing this data may simply involve keeping or copying it (or sometimes taking pictures of it) and reflecting on what it tells you about student learning and the effectiveness of your teaching.

### Teacher-as-Researcher Journal, Teacher Documents

Your teacher education program has no doubt emphasized the importance of reflection in teaching. Thinking deeply and carefully about who your students are or will be, what their challenges and strengths may be, who you are and what you do as a teacher, difficulties you encounter, potential solutions to those difficulties, and a host of other issues is critical to navigating the complex reality that today's classrooms present. Reflection is therefore another critically meaningful potential qualitative data source.

Capturing reflective data involves writing it down in a journal and reflecting on what you have written. For teachers engaged in action research, this journal is not just a teacher journal, but a teacher-as-researcher journal. Weaved throughout much of your reflective journal writing will be information useful for thinking about your action research project.

You should start a teacher-as-researcher journal now if you don't already have one! In it, you should include reflections on your progress in developing an action research project so far. Reflect on your search for a topic, reflect on how each thing you learn along the way influences your emerging action research project, and continue writing about your thoughts and experiences throughout all the stages of your action research project.

You probably made the connection from our discussion of documents above that your teacher-as-researcher journal is a form of document. There are lots of other documents created by or for teachers that are potentially meaningful qualitative data sources. Some of the obvious ones include lesson plans, grading rubrics, content standards and objectives, student IEPs (Individualized Education Programs), textbooks, concrete manipulatives, Web sites, and other educational materials. This is by no means a complete list, and anything created by or for teachers to help them do what they do can be considered a "teacher document" and, therefore, a potential qualitative data source. Capturing these data sources simply involves keeping and reflecting on them.

### Observation, Field Notes, and Other Records

Just as reflection is emphasized in almost every teacher education program, observation is similarly important. Good teachers are great observers of students; seasoned and experienced "kid watchers." They are able to recognize both individual student needs and group or classroom dynamics as they look and listen while teaching. What teachers see and hear is another great potential source of qualitative data.

This source is a little more challenging to capture than those we have discussed so far. Teachers develop a great deal of wisdom and knowledge as they work with students, but they often have difficulty explaining how they know what they know. A teacher is likely to say, "I just know," when asked how they know a particular teaching strategy is working well for a particular student. This is because they often learn implicitly from their work in classrooms without explicitly capturing data for reflection and action. One of the powerful things action research allows teachers to do is to develop more detailed and specific understanding of how observation data supports much of what they "just know."

The challenge with capturing observation data is that whatever you do cannot interfere with teaching, and writing down what you see takes your attention away from your teaching. If you are not teaching yourself and can devote all your attention to capturing observational data, then you can take traditional qualitative field notes where 100 percent of your attention is devoted to capturing the details of what is going on at any given moment.[2] Field notes may be feasible for observations of your host teacher before you are teaching full time yourself, or they may even be feasible during times when your students work independently.

When traditional field notes are not feasible (which will be often), other systems for capturing snippets of observational data may be more manageable. Anecdotal records, running records, behavior logs, and other approaches may fit your needs. While the details of capturing each of these types of data are beyond the scope of this chapter,[3] the essence of each is that some observation data for some students is recorded as it happens. It may be just a brief observation jotted down quickly every so often as you teach. At the very least, you can record reflections based on what you observed earlier in the day in your teacher-as-researcher journal at the end of the day.

Keep in mind, though, that the further away in time and space your reflections are recorded, the less accurate and detailed your memory will be. Still, capturing some observational data during your work in the classroom allows you to reflect on it later and to recognize how what you see and hear in the classroom helps you understand links between what you do as a teacher and your students' learning.

### Interviews and Focus Group

Teachers talk to students, students talk to teachers. Have any of your methods courses discussed the Socratic Method?[4] It wouldn't be much of a stretch to say that asking good questions and getting students talking about their knowledge in order to teach and to assess learning has been a hallmark of education as long as there have been teachers and learners. When done one-on-one and face-to-face, we call this an interview.

Asking questions of groups of students where everyone is expected to answer each question is called a *focus group*. Sometimes this type of potential qualitative data is best captured through observation approaches. However, when a preplanned question-and-answer session is involved, the task of capturing this data may not be as complex as observations of less structured conversations. On one hand, you can determine the questions you expect to ask ahead of time so that you only need to capture the answers, and it is more natural in that kind of interaction to be writing down what you hear. On the other hand, you can consider whether video or audio recording would work well so that you can transcribe the answers later.

Audio is usually enough for an interview, but in a focus group where multiple people are speaking (often at the same time) it is helpful to have a video record. Before doing so, you have to make sure that recording students is permitted by your school and university. Also, when considering recording, be sure to think about whether it is likely to change the way your students behave; bringing a video camera into a classroom is often disruptive if students aren't already used to seeing it there.

### Open-Ended Surveys

The same questions you might ask in an interview or focus group could be put on paper to form open-ended survey questions. Keep in mind that these are not simple yes or no or multiple-choice questions; we'll cover those more under quantitative data sources. Instead, these are questions that require students to write extended answers and to focus on explaining what they know and how they know it, or to focus on describing their feelings, attitudes, opinions, and so forth. These questions are especially useful when you don't really know what kinds of answers you will get and so you want in-depth individualized explanations from your students.

The great benefit to surveys over interviews and focus groups is that they are much easier to capture. Your students complete a document that captures the data for you. However, it is important to think about how likely students are to give you detailed and thoughtful responses when faced with a nearly blank piece of paper as compared to talking face-to-face with you. Younger students tend to give less expanded answers as their limited literacy skills often interfere with expressing themselves.[5] Interviews and focus groups are often much better for getting students talking and therefore provide richer data even though that data is more challenging to capture.

Once again, you need to think about what sources might provide the most meaningful data and how feasible it will be for you to capture that data without disrupting your teaching.

## POTENTIAL QUANTITATIVE DATA SOURCES

Quantitative data sources are more easily captured with numbers. Again, this is nothing more than a useful oversimplification. If it hasn't happened already, as you read through this section you will certainly notice overlap between qualitative and quantitative data sources. Several of the data sources already discussed have quantitative elements to them.

In reality, almost all data sources can provide both quantitative and qualitative information. When you focus on numerical information (such as number of items correct, how many students fall into different categories, or how many times certain students engage in certain behaviors), then you are capturing quantitative data. You should not expect the following to be a complete list of all possible quantitative sources, but you can expect that these are the most commonly used sources in action research studies.

## Teacher-Made Tests and Grading Rubrics

You are probably looking at the heading for this section thinking that we already covered this under student and teacher documents . . . and you are right when you are focused on the qualitative elements of these documents. However, much of the information typically garnered from tests, quizzes, and rubric scores is numerical and, therefore, quantitative.

For the most part, the documents themselves do not determine which kind of data source you capture. Instead, you decide whether to capture and reflect on the qualitative elements or to focus instead on elements such as the number or percentage of correct items, rubric scores for particular elements of an assignment, or other quantitative elements.

When you focus on a numerical summarization of student learning, it becomes relatively easy to compare scores across students and across time. Capturing this data involves using a scoring system to grade student work and then reflecting on what students' scores tell you about your teaching and your impact on your students' learning. The good news is that this is naturally part of your teaching; you would be grading student work and thinking about what their grades tell you regardless of whether or not you were doing action research.

## Standardized Tests and School Records

There are a wide variety of assessments, records, and other documents that can provide numerical information to you as a teacher. With the current push for accountability and standardized testing, there is almost no classroom you could be placed in where you would not have standardized test scores to interpret for each of your students, for subgroups of your students, and for your class as a whole.

Similarly, other school records such as enrollment, attendance, IEP status, and free- or reduced-lunch eligibility can provide important contextual information once you learn who in your school can provide you access to them. All of these can be thought of as documents in the sense that we have been using that word. As such, they are potential sources of both qualitative and quantitative data.

The critical task for you, teacher-as-researcher, is to determine how to capture information from these documents that will be both meaningful and feasible to reflect upon as you teach.

## Observational Checklists and Tally Sheets

One of the ways to make capturing observational data more feasible is to focus on quantitative elements of what occurs. Rather than trying to capture what is going on with narrative description, you focus instead on how many times or how often certain behaviors or events occur. For instance, if you have students working in groups and you have a set of target group behaviors (all members participate, group stays on task, etc.), then you can simply put a check mark for each group next to the target behaviors they display.

You could even have multiple points throughout the group work time when you assess each group. The number of groups or number of students displaying each targeted behavior at various times becomes information about how well the strategy of using groups is functioning. This rapid way of capturing observational data makes it much more feasible to do while teaching and maintains much of the value from direct real-time observation.

## Forced-Choice Surveys

You read above that open-ended survey items are not questions with simple yes or no or multiple-choice answers and that open-ended survey questions are most useful when you don't really know how students will answer them. But if you know that there are really only a limited number of categories that students' answers will fall into, then you can create closed-ended or forced-choice survey items.

Your focus with these types of questions is to find out how many students fall into each of a set of predetermined categories. These kinds of surveys are sometimes called *Likert-type* and are most often used for attitude or opinion polling.[6] Capturing this sort of data involves creating the items and asking students to complete the survey. Once you look at how many students fall into each category, you can reflect on what this tells you about the impact of your teaching on your students. You can even use the same set of forced-choice survey items multiple times to see how students' answers change over time.

## PUTTING IT TOGETHER

As you review the various data sources in figure 2.2, you no doubt recognize that student work samples, documents, surveys, observations, and tests contain both qualitative and quantitative information, so it is up to you to decide what type of data to focus on and capture. The more summary nature of most quantitative data tends to ease comparison across groups of students and across time or comparison to a set standard of performance.

At the same time, quantitative comparison may mask important details of differences among individual students or meaningful aspects of the contexts within which learning occurs. Quantitative data are in some ways easier to collect, grade, and display. These benefits are balanced by their not providing as deep and rich contextual information as qualitative sources.

We hope you will recognize that you do not have to decide on only one type. Instead, we encourage you to include some of both so that the richness and depth of qualitative sources can be augmented by the consistency and comparability of quantitative sources. We'll briefly introduce two terms to expand on this idea: *mixed methods* and *triangulation*.

## UTILIZING A MIXED METHODS APPROACH

*Mixed methods*[7] is a term used for research that draws on the strengths of both qualitative and quantitative approaches to doing research in order to minimize the weaknesses and capitalize on the strengths of each single approach. The basic idea is that more can be learned about whatever you are studying if you include multiple data sources and multiple perspectives.

A related term, *triangulation*, is based on the metaphor of locating something in space. Think of one of those spy movies where they find someone's

| Qualitative Sources | Quantitative Sources |
| --- | --- |
| Student Work Samples, Student Documents | Teacher-made Tests and Grading Rubrics |
| Teacher-as-Researcher Journal, Teacher Documents | Standardized Tests and School Records |
| Observation, Field Notes, and Other Records | Observational Checklists and Tally Sheets |
| Interviews and Focus Groups | Forced Choice Surveys |
| Open-Ended Surveys | |

**Figure 2.2.   Potential Types of Data for Your Action Research**

location by tracking their cell phone. This requires two different locations that can point to where the signal from the spy's phone is coming from. Once you have that, you can form a triangle pointing to where the spy is hiding. A similar process can work for you in your action research project. If you have multiple sources of data, both qualitative and quantitative, both teacher and student perspectives, helping you understand the impact of your teaching strategies, then you will have a much broader and deeper understanding of your impact on your students.

In some ways, more sources of data are better, but be careful not to take that kind of thinking too far because you need to be able to capture and reflect on your data without interfering with your teaching. The trick is to find a balance between including multiple sources to increase your understanding and not including so many sources that data collection interferes with teaching and learning.

## UNDERSTANDING DATA AS YOUR PROJECT UNFOLDS

At this stage, it is critical that you do not just throw all your data in a box and save it to look at once you are done with your action research. One of the most powerful things action research has going for it is the opportunity it gives you to reflect on things as they happen and make real-time course corrections—to react to your initial understandings of your data and help your students learn. This mindset is sometimes called *interim analysis* (Huberman & Miles, 1994), analysis in the middle as your project unfolds.

Interim analysis involves paying attention to data as it comes in to make day-to-day teaching decisions, but it does not involve exhaustive, systematic, and time-consuming approaches to data analysis used in traditional research designs. It is important to remember that learning to teach well is your first priority, and action research should support that focus without impeding your ability to teach.

Interim analysis, or analysis as you teach full time, will not be as systematic and comprehensive as analyses you do after your data has been collected. If you tried to do those deeper, more comprehensive analyses while also teaching full time (probably for the first time), your teaching would likely suffer. It is just too much to do. Instead, your focus for understanding your data as your project unfolds should be completely consistent with what good teachers do regardless of whether or not they are engaged in action research. Your focus should be on understanding your data broadly and reflecting on how your developing understanding can help you make decisions about what and how to teach tomorrow, the next day, or next week.

There is one important way that understanding data as an action research project unfolds differs from what teachers who are not engaged in action research do. You have, or will have, one or more guiding questions for your action research project, but teachers who are not doing action research usually do not have such an explicit set of focusing questions. Throughout your thinking and trying to understand your data at this stage, you need to stay focused on these guiding questions.

Rather than trying to learn everything that can be learned about the data you capture, ask yourself how that data gives you some insight into your guiding questions.

Each guiding question will have a component focused on a student-learning need and a component focused on a teaching or instructional strategy. Captured data may help you understand something related to only a part of one of your guiding questions or it may be related to the whole; either way, keeping your guiding questions in mind as you reflect on your data and how you will teach upcoming lessons will ensure that your action research is productive.

Figure 2.3 describes a real-life sample from a teacher candidate we worked with.[8] Notice how Courtney utilized data sources that fit naturally with her teaching, how her interim analyses helped her make day-to-day teaching decisions, and how it all related directly to her guiding questions.

If you select data sources to capture natural parts of your teaching, striving to understand your data while teaching will not be additional work on top of your teaching; it will be a part of your teaching, something you would do anyway to help you understand how best to help your students. Student work, observation notes, interview data, survey answers, and standardized test results all have to be looked at by any teacher who uses them to evaluate how well their students are "getting" what they are teaching.

Interim analysis simply involves looking at these kinds of data (whether captured qualitatively or quantitatively) and reflecting on what you see within the context of your guiding questions. Your reflections should be written in your teacher-as-researcher journal and should focus on what the data seem to say about student learning and the impact of your teaching strategies. Rather than worrying about how to graphically display trends or calculate statistics at this point, focus on your overall impressions and whether you can think of ways to improve your instruction in areas where students don't seem to be responding as you had hoped.

In addition to thinking about how your data informs your instruction, you should also reflect on how well your data sources seem to be capturing useful information and how feasible collecting data is now that you are face-to-face with the realities of full-time teaching. Action research is about action, so you do not have to stick with your original plans when things don't seem to be working well. This applies as much to your research

Courtney's Guiding Questions: "How does integrating the Arts into a 6th grade social studies classroom increase student participation and motivation?" and, "How does increased participation and motivation lead to greater academic achievement?"

| Sample Data Sources | Interim Analysis |
| --- | --- |
| Forced Choice Survey | An informal online Multiple Intelligence evaluation was given to students at the start of the study in order to understand students' interests and current areas of strength. Results from the Multiple Intelligence evaluations were used as a guide to create diverse and engaging lesson plans emphasizing students' areas of strength, their individual multiple intelligences. |
| Teacher-as Researcher Journal | Courtney spoke daily with students regarding how they felt about lessons and changes going on in the classroom. She kept a reflective teaching journal to record these conversations, including daily notes on how each activity went and if any modifications should be made for future lessons. |
| Open-ended and Forced Choice Surveys | At the end of each lesson, students completed a "Rate this Lesson" card using a 1-10 scale and including written feedback regarding their least and most favorite aspects of that lesson or activity. The students' ratings and feedback were incorporated into subsequent lessons. |
| Student Work Samples | Students' term grades were based on a wide variety of assessment types. Three big projects (where students had choice as to how to represent their learning) were graded using rubrics specific to the type of project turned in. Tests, quizzes, workbook pages, and graphic organizers allowed students to earn points, as did participation in classroom activities and discussion. |

Courtney reflected daily on lessons taught and data collected, using those reflections to plan subsequent lessons. Student input was highly valued as a guide to develop lessons that would be both engaging and meaningful to the students. Based on "Rate this Lesson" scores and students' written comments, lessons that received the highest ratings were grouped to find common threads. If most students did not like a particular activity or assignment and participation was low on that day, that activity was removed from subsequent lesson plans.

**Figure 2.3.   Interim Analysis Focused by Action Research Question**

---

## Self-assessment sheet #1

Name: _____
Date: _____
Quick Reads Title: _____

What did you notice about your reading?
_____
_____
_____
_____

What were some of the problems you had that slowed you down?
_____
_____
_____
_____

How could you improve for the next time you read?
_____
_____
_____
_____

Where there any words you did not know?
_____

If so, what were they? Put a star next to the word you had the
most trouble with.
_____
_____
_____

---

Figure 2.4.  Sample Survey

plan as it does to your teaching strategies. If something is not working, try
something else.

Melissa, an intern, provides a good example of using interim analysis to
make revisions to her research plan. She initially included an open-ended
survey as a data source (as shown in figure 2.4). Third grade students who
struggled with reading fluency would write about their difficulties each day.

---

### Self-Assessment Sheet

Name: _____  WPM: _____

Date: _____  Quick Reads Title: _____

**Read each question. Check all of the answers that apply to you.**

1. What did you notice about your reading this week?
   - o I had more difficulty this week.
   - o I read more smoothly with fewer mistakes.
   - o I read the passage correctly with no mistakes.

2. What were some of the problems you had that slowed down your reading?
   - o recognizing punctuation marks
   - o new vocabulary words
   - o repeated words/parts of a sentence
   - o added words that were not in the passage
   - o left out words
   - o took long pauses while reading
   - o lost my place while reading
   - o voice level (read too softly)
   - o intonation/expression
   - o pacing (read too slow/read too fast)
   - o reading at the target rate of one-minute

3. What were some of the strengths you had?

   - o recognizing punctuation marks
   - o recognizing new vocabulary words
   - o did not repeat as many words
   - o did not add as many words
   - o did not leave out as many words
   - o did not pause for a long time
   - o voice level
   - o intonation/expression
   - o pacing
   - o reading at the target rate of one-minute

   | Words I need to practice: |
   | :--- |
   | _____ |
   | _____ |
   | _____ |

---

**Figure 2.5. Sample Forced Choice Survey**

As Melissa began collecting this data, she soon realized that students were writing very little and it took them a long time to write what they did. She had developed a rubric to score their written responses, but their responses were so short that their scores did not seem to match their learning. The result was that her data was not very informative and collecting that data took away too much instructional time.

Meantime, Melissa had been talking with her students about mistakes they made while reading so she had a good idea of common difficulties they shared. Melissa wisely revised her data source so that rather than writing in response to open-ended questions, students selected one of several common difficulties using a forced-choice format (see figure 2.5). They were able to complete the revised surveys quickly so that Melissa had more time for teaching.

## UNDERSTANDING DATA AFTER
## YOU'VE FINISHED COLLECTING IT

When you reach this stage, you will have completed your data collection and have more time to devote to processing, reflecting on, and understanding your data. If you took our advice in the beginning stages, you included only data sources that fit naturally into your teaching, reflected on your data as it came in, kept a detailed reflective teacher-as-researcher journal capturing your interim analyses, and now have at least general ideas of the main things you learned through action research. Your focus should turn now to organizing, interpreting, and displaying your data to both increase your own understanding and to effectively communicate what you learned in ways that will be convincing to others.

To help you think about how to understand your data now that you are ready for more comprehensive and systematic analyses, we will characterize types of data along two dimensions. Figure 2.6 provides examples of data types that fall into the categories defined by these two dimensions. The first of these, qualitative (narrative and nonnarrative) versus quantitative data types, you will recognize from our discussion above. The second, developmental versus one-time or "snapshot" data needs a little more discussion.

|  | One-time Snapshot | Developmental |
|---|---|---|
| Qualitative, Narrative | Field notes from an observation of your host teacher before beginning student teaching | Daily student journal entries about how much they did or did not like that day's activities |
| Qualitative, Non-narrative | Photographs of school building, computer lab, and playground | Clay sculptures made by students before and after teaching a unit |
| Quantitative | Student performance on state mandated standardized tests | Teacher-made quizzes given at the end of each week |

**Figure 2.6.  Data Examples Differing Along Two Dimensions**

### Snapshot Data

Snapshot data is collected only at a single point in time. This type of data is very useful for understanding the context within which you are teaching. Notice that the three examples in figure 2.6 for one-time snapshot data would allow you to reflect on context at the classroom level with preteaching observation field notes, to reflect on context at the schoolwide level with photographs of the facilities, and to reflect on context at the classroom and student level with high stakes testing data. Each of these kinds of information could be incorporated into teaching decisions, but they do not allow you to think about how what you taught in a particular lesson impacted student learning across time. Understanding contextual data from one-time snapshots differs from understanding developmental data.

The focus for snapshot data is to understand how the context described by this data impacts your students' behavior, learning, and/or attitudes, as well as how that context impacts you as their teacher.

Developmental data is collected at multiple points across time. Developmental data gives you the ability to look across time and see if your students' learning, attitudes, and so on change. The focus for developmental data is to understand how what you do in the classroom on a daily basis relates to changes in your students' behavior, learning, and/or attitudes.

Notice that the three examples for developmental data in figure 2.6 would allow you to understand which teaching strategies students' enjoyed, students' ability to create based on their developing understandings, and how your teaching impacted student achievement. You might recognize that the closer together the times you collect this data become, the more fine-grained or closer to real-time your understanding of the connections between your teaching and student performance will be. But don't forget that your action research data collection has to be feasible while full-time teaching, so be careful not to try and do so much data collection that it interferes with your teaching.

One approach that has worked well for some teacher candidates has been to focus their more intensive data collection and analysis on subgroups of students rather than on all the students they teach. This may be particularly useful for secondary teachers who often work with more than a hundred students each day. We are not advocating control or comparison group approaches where some students get the beneficial treatment while others do not. Leave those types of research designs to traditional researchers, you are doing action research.

You could not ethically withhold from some children a teaching strategy you think might help them. Instead, we are suggesting that while you use your teaching strategies with all students, you include focused data collection and analysis for only a subset. Identifying this subset does not need to follow random-sampling procedures used in traditional research designs.

Those approaches ensure that every potential member of the population you are studying (such as all third graders in your school) have a chance of being in your subset with the goal of making that subset representative of the larger population. But in action research you are not focused on the larger population, you are focused on your classroom.

Instead of random sampling, you should select your sample purposefully so that those students you focus on are most likely to allow you to accomplish the goals you have for your action research. For example, you might select a relatively small number of students at low, medium, and high levels of initial performance.

If your goals include understanding how to individualize instruction for students at these different performance levels, then this purposeful selection will help you accomplish that goal. This selection could be based on one-time snapshot data such as previous standardized test scores that you collect at the beginning of your project and in consultation with your host teacher. While you would not change your instructional strategies for the selected students, you might focus any more intensive data collection strategies (such as observations or interviews) on these students. You might also use only data from these focus students when you do your more focused analyses after your data are collected.

A word or two about using computers to help you understand your data is in order before we move on. There is a wide variety of sophisticated software applications available to help analyze qualitative and quantitative data for research purposes.[9] However, it is important to remember that none of these "does it for you." That is, there is no substitute for you carefully going through and thinking about your data as you analyze it. Additionally, many of you will not have easy access to these more sophisticated programs.

Most of you have access to a word-processing program such as Microsoft Word and a general spreadsheet application such as Microsoft Excel. These relatively general purpose computer applications are surprisingly helpful as supports for analyzing and displaying quantitative and qualitative data. While a nuts-and-bolts explanation of how to use these programs for understanding your data is beyond the scope of this chapter,[10] we will present some general techniques utilizing these programs. In all cases, similar analyses could be accomplished by hand, but the general availability of computers with these general purpose applications makes such hand-cranked options relatively obsolete.

## UNDERSTANDING QUALITATIVE NARRATIVE DATA

Remember the different types of qualitative data sources displayed in figure 2.2? The vast majority of those will be narrative data. That is, they will be text, words on a page. In fact, even those data sources that are initially non-narrative (videos, photographs, objects students create, etc.) will need to be described and interpreted in narrative form (although they may additionally be presented visually).

There are many different approaches to qualitative data analysis for various research traditions that are beyond the scope of this chapter. While each could be applied in action research, we suggest a general qualitative analysis approach that will allow you to feasibly understand your qualitative data. The essence of qualitative data analysis is the exploration or discovery of themes or categories in your data. Throughout this entire process, be sure to keep your guiding questions firmly in mind because it is these questions you are trying to answer by understanding your data.

### Narrative Data Analysis

Your task begins when you have assembled all the various pieces of qualitative data you believe are relevant for your action research project. This tends to be a very large pile of documents. You do not need to analyze everything you have in minute detail, but you should begin by reading through all of it together to get a good sense of what you have.[11] If you have clearly described how each data source relates to each of your guiding questions, you can deal with each question one at a time. Start with a single data source for a single guiding question. You will eventually move to the other data sources and other questions following a similar strategy.

We will use the examples from figure 2.6 to work through analyzing narrative qualitative data. Field notes generated from an observation of your host teacher before you start teaching might help you think about the context you will be stepping into when you teach. If these are typed into a word-processing program, then you can easily convert the narrative data into a 3-column table so that you can put line numbers in the first column, notes to yourself about the data in the second column, and the data itself in the third column (see figure 2.7).

Any narrative data in electronic format can be treated in this same way regardless of whether it is based on field notes or any other qualitative data source. If it is not feasible to put your data into electronic format, a similar approach can be developed for hard copy data by making copies and annotating them with labels as described below. As you read through your narrative data, the process involves trying to describe very succinctly in a few words the main essence of each statement. These succinct statements can be called *categories* or *labels*.

Developing categories or labels that help you answer your guiding questions can take some time. Do not expect the first set of labels you use to be the one you will stick with. Instead, go through applying a set of labels that

| Line #'s | Categories | Narrative from field notes |
|----------|-----------|---------------------------|
| 1. | learning environment | When I first come into the room, I notice a lot of colorful pictures and posters on the walls. Most of these seem related to language arts, but a few are mathematics. |
| 2. | classroom management | The students are milling around and the teacher says loudly "Anyone not sitting quietly in their seats might miss some recess if they don't hear me explain what we're doing this morning!" |
| 3. | learning environment | I note the organization of the desks into four rows with about 8 desks each, all facing forward. |

**Figure 2.7. Sample Field Notes Formatted for Qualitative Analysis**

make sense to you, and then look over what you have done to think about whether you might want to change it. You may want to give more than one label to a particular statement, and you should feel free to do so. It will be helpful at that point to pull together all of the portions of narrative data that have the same label.

Using the data in figure 2.7, you might pull together all statements that you labeled as "learning environment." Looking at that data, then you might decide that there are different aspects of the learning environment that are worth thinking about differently so you will need to develop separate labels for each of those and go back through the data to apply those labels. This is a cyclical process that you should continue until you feel like the labels you are using work well to help you understand what this data says about the guiding question you are currently focused on. For this example, you might eventually develop an understanding of several different aspects of the learning environment within which you did your student teaching.

The same general process should be applied to looking at developmental data such as student journal entries across time. The main difference here is that you want to be able to see how things changed, not just what was going on at one time. Once you understand how things changed (or didn't change), then you can relate that to the different things you did in your teaching across time to get an idea of what impact you may have had on your students.

For developmental qualitative data, we suggest using only data from the first day to generate a preliminary set of categories or labels. In our example, that would be the first set of journal entries. Once labels have been applied to that first set, apply those labels to each consecutive day, and then look to see whether there are parts of the narrative data from later days that were not labeled. If there are parts without labels that *you* think include important information, then you'll need to develop new labels for that data. These new labels may be particularly illuminating because they will be examples of things that did not occur in the earlier data.

Once you have moved through all the data across time, you can look at how all the narrative data with a particular label does or does not seem to change across time. Gathering all the data with the same label together and reading through it often helps you recognize things you would not see otherwise. As you work through this process, continue adding to your teacher-as-researcher journal. Write and reflect on what you are learning along the way so that you don't forget it.

Go back to our example, and let's assume you have a guiding question related to the effectiveness of workbook and hands-on activities. Perhaps you created labels for "negative toward workbooks" and "positive toward hands-on activity" while coding the first journal entries. Then later journal entries required you to create a "positive toward workbooks" label. After looking across all the journal entries you might find that there were more "positive toward workbooks" statements relative to negative ones as the incidence of "positive toward hands-on activity" also increased across time. You might then relate this to changes in your teaching strategy where you increased the amount of hands-on activities while decreasing the amount of workbook activities. You might then make a preliminary conclusion that students can enjoy workbooks as long as they are not overused.

## UNDERSTANDING QUALITATIVE NONNARRATIVE DATA

As we mentioned earlier, nonnarrative data will need to be described in narrative form so that you can write about it in your reflective journal and talk about it when it comes time to communicate what you have learned. Look back at figure 2.6 for examples of this kind of data.

Photographs should be described focusing on what you think they reveal about your school context. Describe sculptures, dioramas, or other nonnarrative student work products, focusing on what you think they reveal about student knowledge, learning, attitudes, interests, and so forth. Be sure to take pictures of these three-dimensional student work products so that you can show them to people when you share what you learned through action research.

Whenever qualitative nonnarrative data are developmental in nature, be sure to look for and describe any changes across time. Some nonnarrative data lends itself well to transcription, such as audio tapes of student conversations or students reading aloud. Other nonnarrative data, such as videotapes of lessons you taught or of students working in groups, can be converted into narrative data by taking field notes while watching them; describe what you see and what is said. Those descriptions and transcriptions can then be analyzed using the process described in the previous section for narrative data. Throughout all of this, remember to frequently review your guiding questions to be sure your focus remains consistent.

## UNDERSTANDING QUANTITATIVE DATA

Review once again our examples of quantitative data in figure 2.6. Quantitative data that provides snapshots is useful for understanding your students' incoming performance, academic preparation, and class-, school-, or community-level contexts. In addition to standardized test scores, this data might include the number of students eligible for free or reduced lunch, the number of students with various IEP statuses, enrollment and attendance data, disciplinary referrals, school-funding data, and a host of other possibilities. What all these have in common is that they contain information from one point in time rather than providing information about how what is being measured changed from day-to-day or week-to-week.

Analyzing quantitative snapshot data often includes paying careful attention to subgroups. Rather than looking at change across time as in developmental data, you may be interested in differences among specific groups. For example, figure 2.8 is a standardized test report for a high school in West Virginia. This is the kind of data No Child Left Behind mandates be reported for all schools nationwide so you can be sure something similar will be available to you. Notice that the county this school is in (Monongalia) performs well above average in science for the state, and this school's average overall is even higher than that of the county.[12] If you were a special education teacher in this school, though, you might have cause for concern because that subgroup of students scored only 704, well below even the "economically disadvantaged" students who scored 715. Depending on the focus of your action research and your guiding questions, different subgroup comparisons will be more or less relevant.

Information such as that in the lower portion of figure 2.8 can be particularly helpful to analyze even before your project begins. This section of the standardized test report describes student performance on items related to specific content standards and objectives. If available, this kind of information can help you think about what areas your students are likely to struggle in. For example, while more than 90 percent of students in this school scored at or above mastery in Science as Inquiry, Science Subject Matter/

| Science | Performance Levels | | | | | | | | | | | | | | Grade Level Mastery Data | | | | |
|---|---|---|---|---|---|---|---|---|---|---|---|---|---|---|---|---|---|---|---|
| | Number of Students Tested* | Distinguished | | Above Mastery | | Mastery | | Partial Mastery | | Novice | | At or Above Mastery | | Below Mastery | | Mean Scale Score |
| | | N | % | N | % | N | % | N | % | N | % | N | % | N | % | |
| WEST VIRGINIA | 19266 | 2111 | 11 | 6470 | 34 | 8247 | 43 | 2074 | 11 | 384 | 2 | 16828 | 87 | 2458 | 13 | 713 |
| MONONGALIA | 757 | 173 | 23 | 280 | 37 | 249 | 33 | 52 | 7 | 3 | 0 | 702 | 93 | 55 | 7 | 727 |
| MORGANTOWN N HIGH | 396 | 110 | 28 | 150 | 38 | 114 | 29 | 22 | 6 | 0 | 0 | 374 | 94 | 22 | 6 | 732 |
| **Gender** | | | | | | | | | | | | | | | | |
| Female | 185 | 43 | 23 | 72 | 39 | 65 | 35 | 6 | 3 | 0 | 0 | 180 | 97 | 6 | 3 | 729 |
| Male | 210 | 67 | 32 | 78 | 37 | 49 | 23 | 16 | 8 | 0 | 0 | 194 | 92 | 16 | 8 | 734 |
| **Race/Ethnicity** | | | | | | | | | | | | | | | | |
| Asian/Pacific Islander | 13 | 8 | 62 | 4 | 31 | 1 | 8 | 0 | 0 | 0 | 0 | 13 | 100 | 0 | 0 | 756 |
| Black | 22 | 3 | 14 | 10 | 45 | 5 | 23 | 4 | 18 | 0 | 0 | 18 | 82 | 4 | 18 | 717 |
| Hispanic | N Count below 10 | | | | | | | | | | | | | | | |
| American Indian | 0 | 0 | 0 | 0 | 0 | 0 | 0 | 0 | 0 | 0 | 0 | 0 | 0 | 0 | 0 | |
| White (not Hispanic) | 354 | 97 | 27 | 135 | 38 | 106 | 30 | 16 | 5 | 0 | 0 | 338 | 95 | 16 | 5 | 732 |
| Other | 0 | 0 | 0 | 0 | 0 | 0 | 0 | 0 | 0 | 0 | 0 | 0 | 0 | 0 | 0 | |
| Students with Disabilities | 46 | 4 | 9 | 8 | 17 | 22 | 48 | 12 | 26 | 0 | 0 | 34 | 74 | 12 | 26 | 704 |
| LEP Students | N Count below 10 | | | | | | | | | | | | | | | |
| Migrant | 0 | 0 | 0 | 0 | 0 | 0 | 0 | 0 | 0 | 0 | 0 | 0 | 0 | 0 | 0 | |
| Economically Disadvantaged | 104 | 16 | 15 | 28 | 27 | 47 | 45 | 13 | 13 | 0 | 0 | 92 | 88 | 13 | 13 | 715 |

MORGANTOWN HI

| Science Content Standards | Number of Students Tested* | Grade Level Mastery of Content Standards | | | | |
|---|---|---|---|---|---|---|
| | | At or Above Mastery Level | | Below Mastery Level | | Mean % Correct |
| | | N | % | N | % | |
| 1. History and the Nature of Science | 396 | 316 | 80 | 80 | 20 | 62 |
| 2. Science as Inquiry | 396 | 366 | 92 | 30 | 8 | 47 |
| 3. Unifying Themes | 396 | 279 | 70 | 117 | 30 | 47 |
| 4. Science Subject Matter/Concepts | 396 | 379 | 96 | 17 | 4 | 62 |
| 5. Scientific Design and Application | 396 | 339 | 86 | 57 | 14 | 67 |
| 6. Science in Personal and Social Persp. | 396 | 373 | 94 | 23 | 6 | 67 |

*Note: Adding all of the percents for a group will equal between 99-101% due to rounding.

**Figure 2.8. Sample State Mandated Standardized Test Report**

Concepts, and Science in Personal and Social Perspectives, 20 percent or more were below mastery level in History and the Nature of Science and Unifying Themes. Clearly, these latter content standards are more likely to be important areas to focus action research studies on if you are interested in science learning.

## Quantitative Developmental Data Analysis

Developmental data gets at the heart of what action research studies are all about. It is here that you can see how student behavior, learning, and attitudes change across time as you teach. You should analyze your quantitative developmental data on both individual student and group levels. How the class as a whole, or a subgroup you have chosen to focus on, changes

| | 10/5/2007 Concrete | 10/12/2007 Virtual | 10/19/2007 Testing | 10/26/2007 Concrete | 11/2/2007 Virtual | **Average** |
|---|---|---|---|---|---|---|
| Caleb | 4 | 6 | 4 | 8 | 10 | 6.4 |
| Riley | 8 | 8 | 6 | 6 | 4 | 6.4 |
| Chloe | 6 | 6 | 4 | 10 | 10 | 7.2 |
| Kristen | 10 | 10 | 6 | 8 | 10 | 8.8 |
| **Average** | 7 | 7.5 | 5 | 8 | 8.5 | 7.2 |

**Figure 2.9.  Sample Quantitative Developmental Data: End of Week Math Quiz Scores across Five Weeks with Alternating Teaching Strategies**

across time is important information. How individual students improve, remain constant, or even lose ground is at least equally important for teachers. At the end of the day, it is on the individual student level that teachers have their most important impact. It is in the lives of individual students that you can make a difference.

Let's return to our example to demonstrate the approach we suggest you follow. Remember that the data source in this example is teacher-made math quizzes at the end of each week. Let's further say you selected four focus students and utilized concrete manipulatives (physical objects) while teaching one week and then used virtual manipulatives (online or computer based) the next, planning to alternate these approaches across several weeks. Let's say further that something happened in week 3 and you were unable to use either approach (maybe that was a week where standardized testing was occurring). So you ended up alternating approaches for weeks one and two, and then again for weeks four and five. You might have quantitative developmental data that looks something like figure 2.9 when entered in Microsoft Excel.

Almost all spreadsheet programs will allow you to calculate an average for each row and column. The exact procedures for doing this differ for every program and change with new versions so we won't detail them here. Someone at your university or school can certainly help you learn to do so if you aren't already able to. Notice that these averages tell you how the group as a whole performed on a particular week's quiz and how an individual student performed across all five weeks. This same approach can be used regardless of how many students you include.

Once you have these averages in addition to the initial individual scores, then you are in a good position to graphically represent trends that will go a long way to helping you understand your quantitative developmental data. If we start by looking at the group as a whole, we could produce a bar chart such as figure 2.10, demonstrating general improvement across time and a small advantage of virtual over concrete manipulatives. Also notice that it is immediately clear that something happened in week 3 that negatively impacted student performance on the quiz. If we hadn't already said stan-

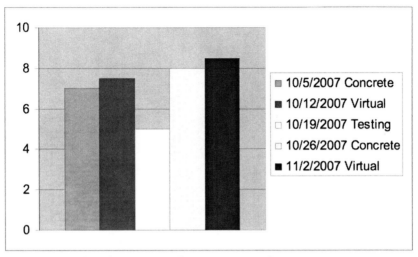

**Figure 2.10. Displaying Group Performance Across Time**

dardized testing interrupted instruction that week, then you would need to search through your teacher-as-researcher journal to try and understand that dip in group level performance.

If you look at the individual student averages across time (figure 2.9), you can see that Caleb and Riley both appeared to be struggling, scoring 64 percent each, compared to Chloe and Kristen. An examination of each of their scores individually across time reveals important information that you would miss if you stayed focused on group averages.

Another type of graph, a line graph with a separate line for each individual student, is very useful for visualizing this. We recommend you start with all students' performance on the same graph to look for patterns yourself. This will be a working graph, but you will immediately realize that it is too busy, too crowded, for presenting what you find to others.

From your working graph, you can then pull out the elements you most want your reader or audience to focus on. This is what we show in figure 2.11, with lines displaying Caleb and Riley's performance across the five weeks of this study. Even though their average performance across time was equal, this graph shows Caleb making good progress, but there is cause for concern in Riley's performance. The main point here is that you should never lose sight of individual students when trying to understand your data. There is a lot you can learn when combining performance across groups of students, but don't let that focus blur your ability to understand individual student data.

Some of you may be wondering what happened to all that stuff you learned in your statistics classes. You recognized the average as the mean,

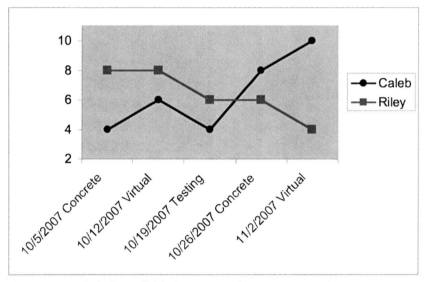

Figure 2.11.   Displaying Individual Student Performance Across Time

but you haven't heard anything about t-tests, ANOVAs, or chi-square analyses. We have purposefully not discussed these statistical tools because many action research projects will not need them.

Many projects, especially those that focus on a small subset of students for focused data collection, simply do not meet the requirements for those statistical tools to be applicable, requirements such as large sample sizes and random sampling. However, there may be occasions when these statistical tools are appropriate for some action research studies. We encourage you to seek out advice from faculty who specialize in traditional research designs and statistical analyses if you think they might apply to your project.

## MIXING, TRIANGULATING, AND DISPLAYING YOUR DATA

There are at least two reasons for you to think about displaying your data: (1) to help you visualize and understand your data better and (2) to help you effectively communicate what you have learned to others.

Your quantitative data can be displayed in tables and charts similar to those we have used in this chapter. Qualitative narrative data is often best displayed by including excerpts or quotations that are good examples of particular categories, or they could be displayed in a table similar to figure 2.6. You can also make a table listing all the categories you developed in analyzing your narrative data and even quantify how many times each category occurs.

Qualitative nonnarrative data can be displayed by including pictures or even video, depending on the format of your report. Just remember that your goal with all data displays should be to help to bring your reader into your action research and to help them understand your data from your perspective.

Before wrapping up this chapter, we want you to take a step back and remember the big picture. We have been discussing analysis for each data source and each type of data separately, and this is the way we suggest you begin your in-depth analysis after your data are collected. But once you have a good understanding of each data source, you also need to look across all data sources.

Remember our discussion earlier of mixed methods and triangulation. We encouraged you to use multiple different data sources to allow for triangulation. It is looking for connections, consistency, and confirmation across different data sources that will give you the greatest understanding of your data. It is displaying consistency (or sometimes lack of consistency) across data sources that will help your readers or audience best understand what you have learned through your action research. For any point you want to make, any particular "thing" you want to be able to say you learned from your action research, you should be able to draw on more than one data source as supporting evidence. This is the essence of triangulation.

Let's stick with the example we used for quantitative developmental data a little longer. Remember that this involved using concrete and virtual manipulatives in teaching mathematics. If you think you see support in the quiz data (figures 2.7 and 2.8) for virtual manipulatives being more effective, then you need to look at other data sources to see if similar support exists there. Perhaps you included open-ended surveys where students told you what they did and did not like about activities each day. Perhaps you included reflections on how each teaching event went in your teacher-as-researcher journal. Perhaps you included worksheets that students completed as they worked with each type of manipulative.

You could analyze all of these developmental sources to see whether there was evidence that students liked virtual manipulatives better, whether the teaching events with virtual manipulatives went better from your perspective, and whether their work demonstrated more efficient learning with virtual manipulatives as compared to their work with concrete manipulatives.

Your focus for this higher-level analysis should be looking for whether there is consistency in what you learned from your earlier analysis of each separate data source. More than likely, you will not find complete consistency across sources, but you will almost always find that you learn more about your teaching and about your students' learning when you examine multiple sources.

Triangulation is especially important for understanding individual student performance. Remember that figure 2.11 provided two different patterns of student performance across time and led to concern that Riley was having difficulty, especially during the final two weeks of data collection. Considering that all of the other students seemed to improve or at least stay relatively stable, as previously shown in figure 2.9, your focus for understanding Riley's challenges might be about looking for how Riley differs from your other focus students.

You should look at all of your developmental data sources to see whether Riley had similar difficulties there or whether there was something specific to the quizzes giving her difficulty. You should also look at any snapshot data to see whether you can find anything about larger contextual issues that might be causing Riley's difficulties. Again, you may not find any clear answers, but as a teacher committed to helping individual students you will want keep searching for ways that you can help Riley improve.

Finally, triangulation is also important if something unusual jumps out when looking at a single data source. We alluded to an example of this earlier. Look again at figure 2.10. Assume this time that nothing obvious was different about week 3, that there was no standardized testing that week. In this case, you would have to try and understand what happened to cause such a dip in student performance that week. Starting with this quantitative data that needs explaining, you should look through other data sources to see if they help you understand it.

A good starting place to peruse your data will always be your teacher-as-researcher journal. Your journal should help you remember what happened that week, what you taught, how the students behaved, any particular events that caught your attention, and so forth.

Other data sources like observations, surveys, and other student work might reveal a lack of interest or particular difficulty with the content. They might reveal that the way you implemented your teaching strategies that week was somehow different or that something in the larger context of the school or community might have had an impact.

Of course, you may not find any clear reason for that dip; you may not have collected the data that would help you explain it. You won't always get clear answers because teaching and learning in real classrooms is messy. But looking for those answers by seeking connections across data sources is the most likely way for you to find those answers if they are in your data. If they simply aren't in your data, it is important to remember that action research is a career-long process and you are just starting out. You will have opportunity throughout your career to study and improve your teaching. If you find a challenging question you cannot answer with this action research study, then you have found a great focus for your next action research study.

You will find that triangulation is, to a large degree, about getting the big picture of what occurred and what you have learned throughout your action research. A good way to think about this, especially when you are at the stage where you need to communicate what you learned to others, is to think about "telling your story." We often advise teacher candidates in the final stage of their action research to take a step back and think about the main things they have learned along the way:

- What do you think you gained from teaching and conducting action research?
- What do you think your students gained from the way you taught them?
- How can you tell the stories of what you learned using both your qualitative and your quantitative data?

If you can find a few main points that convey what you learned, then the next step is to think about how best to tell the story of how you learned those things. Telling that story effectively will involve helping your reader to understand your data and how your data led you through your own story.

## CONCLUSION

We have tried in this chapter to help you figure out (1) what kinds of data to collect, (2) how to reflect on that data as you are collecting it, and (3) how to structure, display, and reflect on your data once you have it. Along the way we have emphasized that you should not lose focus of the guiding questions for your action research, that you should carefully plan so that your data collection will be feasible while you are teaching full time, that you should look for connections across data sources in addition to understanding each source separately, and that you should focus both on groups of students and on individual student performance across time. We hope this will put you in the admirable position of understanding your data so that you can complete your action research and, more important, so that you can guide your reflective teaching practice with data-based decision making.

## QUESTIONS FOR REVIEW AND REFLECTION

1. How does understanding data influence each stage of an action research study differently?

2. What are the most commonly used qualitative data sources in action research studies? What are the most common quantitative sources?
3. Which data sources are most likely to be relevant and feasible for your specific action research study?
4. Define *mixed methods* and *triangulation* in your own words.
5. Explain what your focus should be when conducting interim analysis.
6. How do snapshot and developmental data differ? How can each type inform your action research study?
7. Describe the process for analyzing narrative data. For quantitative developmental data.
8. What are two reasons for displaying data?
9. Why is triangulation important? How can it help you understand your data?

## NOTES

1. If you are wondering why we don't just use the term *student work samples*, it is because we will be using the term *documents* in later sections when they are created by or for teachers and not just when they are created by students.

2. We recommend reading *"Stretching" Exercises for Qualitative Researchers* (Janesick 1998) for activities to strengthen your skills in capturing observation data with field notes.

3. We recommend *Improving Schools through Action Research: A Comprehensive Guide for Educators* (Hendricks 2009) for more detail, especially chapter 5, "Strategies for Collecting Data."

4. www.wikipedia.org has a useful explanation of the Socratic Method if you aren't already familiar with it.

5. Creative ways around this challenge are sometimes effective, such as asking younger children to draw pictures for their answers.

6. For example, How prepared are you to decide which data sources to include in your action research? Circle only one:

Very prepared      Somewhat prepared      Poorly prepared      Unprepared

7. We use the term *mixed methods* because it is best known in the literature even though we prefer *multi-methodological*, which Luttrell (2005) explains as explicitly focused on integrating fuller research perspectives, paradigms, and tool kits rather than simply integrating diverse methods for capturing data.

8. For more detail, see Kosky & Curtis (2008).

9. These include Atlas. ti, Ethnograph, and NVivo among many others for qualitative analyses, and SPSS, SAS, and MINITAB among many others for quantitative analyses.

10. For this nuts-and-bolts treatment of qualitative data analysis, see Hahn (2008).

11. Our approach to qualitative data analysis is a synthesis of our own experiences with preservice teacher action research and suggestions from several qualitative researchers, including Berg (2001), Denzin & Lincoln (2008), Strauss (1987), and Tesch (1990).

12. The state average is 713, the county average is 727, and the school average is 732.

## REFERENCES

Berg, B. L. (2001). *Qualitative research methods for the social sciences*. Needham Heights, MA: Allyn & Bacon.

Denzin, N. & Lincoln, Y. (Eds.) (2008). *Collecting and interpreting qualitative materials* (3rd ed.). Thousand Oaks, CA: Sage.

Hahn, C. (2008). *Doing qualitative research using your computer: A practical guide*. Thousand Oaks, CA: Sage Publications.

Hendricks, C. (2009). *Improving schools through action research: A comprehensive guide for educators*. Needham Heights, MA: Allyn & Bacon.

Huberman, A., & Miles, M. (1994). Data management and analysis methods. In *Handbook of qualitative research* (pp. 428–44). Thousand Oaks, CA: Sage Publications.

Janesick, V. (1998). *"Stretching" exercises for qualitative researchers*. Thousand Oaks, CA: Sage Publications.

Kosky, C., & Curtis, R. (2008). An action research exploration integrating student choice and arts activities in a sixth grade social studies classroom. *Journal of Social Studies Research, 32*(1), 22–27.

Luttrell, W. (2005). Crossing anxious borders: Teaching across the quantitative-qualitative 'divide.' *International Journal of Research and Method in Education, 28*(2), 183–95.

Strauss, A. (1987). *Qualitative analysis for social scientists*. Cambridge, England: Cambridge University Press.

Tesch, R. (1990). *Qualitative research: Analysis Types and Software*. Abingdon, England: Routledge Farmer.

# 3

# Developing an Action Research Project

*Geraldine C. Jenny, EdD, Associate Professor of Education, Elementary Education/Early Childhood Department, Slippery Rock University, Pennsylvania*

*Robert C. Snyder, PhD, Associate Professor of Education, Elementary Education/ Early Childhood Department, Slippery Rock University, Pennsylvania*

## INTRODUCTION

This chapter is designed to guide teacher candidates through the process of conducting action research. The following process can fit any teacher's self-paced timetable and will prove well worth the effort as teachers and their students alike reap the benefits.

By the time you finish reading and thinking about this chapter you will be able to:

- Identify and formulate a research question
- Conduct a literature review and compose a methodology section to guide your action research
- Examine and report on data appropriately
- Sum up your conclusions and implications for other teachers
- Present your action research in a professional format

As you read previously, action research has become a popular format for any teacher who desires to improve their own teaching. Now is the time for you to focus on what is important for you to examine regarding teaching and learning in your own classroom. Action research allows teachers a time-saving way to stay current with research and improve their teaching while enhancing student learning during the busy schedule of the typical teaching year.

A powerful way to understand something new is to see the work produced by other teacher candidates. As you move through this chapter, you will be introduced to exemplary student work samples that will help you see what students just like you have accomplished in their own action research.

## OVERVIEW OF THE PROCESS

In chapter 1 you learned that action researchers generally follow a process such as the one described below to guide their practice:

1. Issue Identification
2. Data Collection
3. Action Planning
4. Plan Activation
5. Outcome Assessment (see chapter 1)

Most teachers tend to focus their action research in an area of academic need. In the approach presented in this chapter, you will see how teacher candidates work with their cooperating teachers to select an area of emphasis in one of the major subject areas of the elementary curriculum (i.e., mathematics, science, social studies, or reading). Although action research can be used to focus on almost anything you choose in the teaching and learning environment, we will not be focusing on topics such as student behavior because the goal of many teacher-training programs is to have you focus your research on teaching strategies that impact student learning.

As you follow some of the action research guidelines provided in this chapter, you will assess students in a content area and plan and teach lessons that target that focus. You will develop an action research proposal and lesson plans, and you will gather assessment data and student work samples that will measure student learning and document the effect of your work with students.

To begin this process, we urge you to have a conference with your cooperating teacher and discuss student performance, content area goals, objectives, and any classroom concerns regarding their students' academic development. Together, identify an academic area or issue of emphasis for the action research project. Try to be specific. For example, "comprehension" is too broad a topic, but, "identifying the letter B" is too narrow a topic. Issue identification will vary, depending upon your own children, in your particular classroom.

Once an area of emphasis has been identified, you will begin to do some research on the topic. You might find yourself looking though course notes, textbooks, professional journals, online resources, or talking with your teacher, colleagues, and professors while identifying possible teaching strategies and assessments related to your course of study. You might even develop new strategies of your own. You will find in the pages ahead that the power and potential of action research lies within you, your students, and your classroom. The following steps will assist you in your work.

## ACTION RESEARCH STEPS

### Step 1: Issue Identification

The first priority you should have when doing action research is to make sure that your research question is open ended. In other words, your question should not have a simple yes or no answer! Deciding upon your question is one of the hardest tasks of the action research project. How you write this question will impact the way you will approach your topic, the type of data to collect, how you will analyze the data, and the ways in which you will report the results of your study.

You may be pondering what approaches there are to developing a good research question. This process may be a bit messy at first. As you write and reflect upon your question, you will find that you revise and refine it often. Remember the reflection-in-action mindset discussed in chapter 1? Utilize your professional resources such as your school and university supervisors, college professors, and other experts in the field. It is not unusual to revise the wording of your question many times throughout the process of the initial question formulation, the review of related literature, and during the planning and procedural phases in writing your paper.

When identifying a possible topic, one approach is to use question stems. These are thought starters that allow you to focus on topics of interest to you related to teaching and learning. Some common questions stems (Hubbard & Powell 1999) to help you get started in thinking and developing a topic of interest include:

- What classroom procedures or activities promote . . . ?
- How does . . . ?
- What issues do students encounter when . . . ?
- What happens when . . . ?

- How can . . . ?
- What is the difference between . . . ?
- How do students . . . ?
- What strategies do students use to . . . ?

Consider the following open-ended statements to help you get started:

- Something I am particularly interested in learning about teaching is . . .
- A content area that I am particularly interested in learning about in classrooms is . . .
- In my classroom teaching, I am bothered by . . .
- I am very curious about . . .
- I desire to . . .
- I would like to make a difference in the classroom by . . .
- If I could change something about teaching or student learning it would be . . .
- I am passionate in wanting to learn about . . .

Keep a journal, such as a teacher-as-researcher journal, as described in the previous chapter and brainstorm a list of things that you wonder about in your classroom. What surprises, concerns, intrigues, or delights you (Hubbard & Powell 1999)? Other strategies to assist you in finding your research question are to consider the following four approaches (Johnson 2003; Sagor 1992):

- Study or evaluate a teaching method or technique in order to determine its effectiveness.
- Identify and investigate a problem to understand what is happening and the possible causes of the problem.
- Examine an area of interest. What are you curious about? What in particular about teaching interests you the most?
- Create a graphic representation, brainstorm and arrange factors, variables, and contexts related to a topic of interest.

Some action research questions developed by previous teacher candidates include:

- How will using a rubric to self-edit a weekly personal narrative impact students' writing skills? (Lauren)
- What is the relationship between the incorporation of the arts into vocabulary instruction and vocabulary achievement? (Alycia)
- How will the use of sight word strategies increase reading fluency? (Melissa)

- How does drill and repetition affect the retention of math multiplication facts? (Jesse)
- How does adding art to a project enhance student academic performance? (Melissa)
- How does the use of graphic organizers impact paragraph writing? (Kimberly)
- What are the impacts of kinesthetic and visual instructional strategies on letter recognition with kindergarten students? (Molly)

While developing an issue to study, keep in mind that

- Key starting words of action research questions are usually "what" or "how," which focus on explanations, reasons, and relationships.
- A good action research question is meaningful to you, possible to do in your classroom, manageable, written in everyday language, and has not already been answered.
- It is concise but is not a yes or no question.
- An appropriate question is one in which you feel commitment and passion.
- It should provide you with an opportunity to grow as a professional while providing you with a deeper understanding of the topic and will definitely lead to other questions.

A final suggestion to aid in refining your research question and to frame your study's introductory paragraph is to develop a problem statement. Use the question development chart below to develop your problem statement. Always come back to what you wonder about and what intrigues you in your classroom. Your problem statement consists of a brief statement that answers the following critical queries that are affected by the question that you select:

1. Who is affected?
2. Who or what is suspected of causing the problem?
3. What kind of problem has been identified?
4. What is your goal for improvement or what will be the outcome if your action has an ideal impact? (Sagor 1992)

Complete the following checklist in figure 3.1 to help you with your issue identification:

**Checklist for Success**
❏ Identify factors, variables, and contexts related to your topic of interest.

| | Possibility #1 | Possibility #2 | Possibility #3 |
|---|---|---|---|
| **List general areas you are interested in here (e.g. math)** | | | |
| **List specific topics under each area (e.g. fractions)** | | | |
| **List the factors that impact the topic listed (e.g. use of manipulatives)** | | | |
| **Write a potential question here (e.g. How does the use of manipulatives impact student understanding of equivalent fractions?)** | Possible Question #1 | Possible Question #2 | Possible Question #3 |

**Figure 3.1.   Question Development Chart**

- ❏ Reflect on the curriculum standards and the strategies you might implement to meet your students' needs.
- ❏ Focus on a subject area where students need improvement.
- ❏ Study the above list of previous successful action research questions.
- ❏ Consider a short list of possible questions you might be interested in researching.
- ❏ Begin to think about who is affected, what the problem is, or what improvement is needed to each of your questions.
- ❏ Generate key words and resources that might offer information on your proposed research questions.
- ❏ Identify possible data that would align with research questions under consideration.
- ❏ Discuss the feasibility and practicality of investigating proposed research questions with your cooperating teacher and university supervisor.
- ❏ Narrow down your short list to one research question that is of interest and worth investigating to you.
- ❏ Refine your question so that it is clearly worded and understandable.
- ❏ Construct a graphic representation of your research question.

### Step 2: Data Collection

There are many data sources that substantiate the need for your study. If you haven't already done so, consider some of these sources to further investigate and substantiate the need to explore your identified issue. An in-depth exploration might cause you to reconsider or modify your research question.

In chapter 1, you learned about using data in action, as you plan and implement your action research. Some data that you might already be using or may wish to further explore might include:

- anecdotal records
- classroom test scores
- standardized test scores
- running records
- parental feedback
- cooperating teacher input
- formal and informal observations

Once you are satisfied that your key question matches your research interests and data-driven needs, be sure your question is aligned with curriculum standards and/or school improvement goals.

## Step 3: Action Planning

As you move forward from here, consider the big picture. You will want your study to be well thought out and planned so that it flows smoothly and avoids potential roadblocks along the way. Consider completing the "Organizing Your Study" flowchart in figure 3.2, as you move through the action-planning step of the action research process. This will help you stay organized.

While action planning, also be sure to remember the collaborative mindset of an action researcher described in chapter 1. Engage in dialogues with your college and school supervisors, other classroom teachers, specialists in the school, as well as your professors on campus. This reflection-in-action experience will surely help you to develop the most useful and effective action plan.

There are three critical considerations for action planning:

1. understanding context features
2. identifying best practices
3. developing research methods

### Understanding Contextual Features

Now that you have revised and refined your question until it matches your classroom data and research issue, it is time to assess how certain

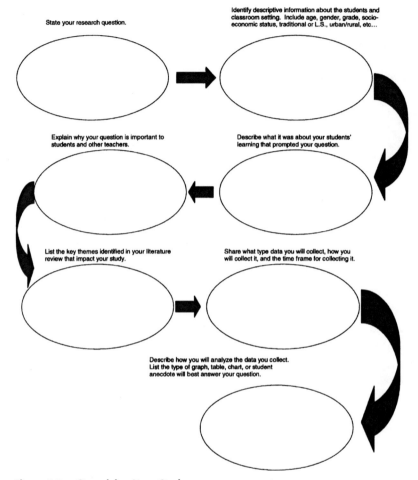

State your research question.

Identify descriptive information about the students and classroom setting. Include age, gender, grade, socio-economic status, traditional or L.S., urban/rural, etc...

Explain why your question is important to students and other teachers.

Describe what it was about your students' learning that prompted your question.

List the key themes identified in your literature review that impact your study.

Share what type data you will collect, how you will collect it, and the time frame for collecting it.

Describe how you will analyze the data you collect. List the type of graph, table, chart, or student anecdote will best answer your question.

**Figure 3.2.  Organizing Your Study**

contextual features might influence your study. Consider the following components as you move forward with your action planning:

- Where was the research conducted?
- What setting and characteristics can be shared regarding your school and students? This should include: the grade level or age ranges, the socioeconomic status (SES) reported as the percentage of free and reduced lunch rates, ethnic composition reported as the percentage of each group represented, gender composition reported as the number of boys and girls, and location reported as urban, rural, or suburban. Most of this information can be located with online school databases such as http://nces.ed.gov/ccd/schoolsearch/ or www.schoolmatters.com/.

- What was the reasoning that ultimately led you to select this particular question?
- Why is it important?
- How will the results impact your teaching?
- How may your study help provide insight into the teaching practices of others?

The following work is excerpted from an action research proposal.

### Exemplary Sample of Student Work: Metacognitive Strategies

#### *Introduction*

*How does explicit instruction with a metacognitive strategy like "Talking to the Text" increase reading comprehension? This question will affect eleven lower-level reading students in the sixth grade at a rural elementary school. There are two differently abled groups and this group is the lower of the two. These students are identified for this reading level through PSSA scores, previous grades, and teacher recommendation.*

*This sixth grade group is comprised of eleven students, eight boys and three girls. Ages ranging from eleven to thirteen years and the levels of cognitive ability are quite varied. The school offers a free breakfast and lunch program, as well as an afterschool tutoring program. The students' socioeconomic background is middle class. For the most part, the students are very well behaved and eager to learn. The learning climate is very relaxed, but classroom management is handled in a firm manner with both punishments corrective discipline and positive rewards.*

*The development of this question arises from my initial observations of students' reading comprehension during small-group discussions of a trade book. Students demonstrated basic proficiency in oral reading to some extent, but most failed to comprehend specifics when asked to retell. It is perplexing to me as a teacher candidate to watch the struggle. My cooperating teacher expressed concern that these students were reading below grade level and might benefit from some type of specific metacognitive strategy.*

*The topic of reading comprehension has traditionally been a fascinating area to explore for educators as they examine the interaction that occurs between the reader and the text. Teachers need to provide scaffolding to struggling readers so that they may develop an awareness of not only what they read, but how and why they read. Purposes need to be established by classroom teachers so that students may see the importance of comprehension as a means of acquiring new information that will benefit them in the future and not just as a means of getting through the current testing situation.*

*The information generated by this study will benefit me as a classroom teacher as well as the students. As these students will be entering high school next year, I feel that they would be well served to improve their reading comprehension in both fiction and expository texts.*

**Checklist for Success**
- ❏ Carefully check grammar, punctuation, and spelling.
- ❏ Use an active voice when writing of the present.
- ❏ Use past tense when writing of events that occurred in the past.
- ❏ Examine the samples of exemplary action-research-paper introductions included in this chapter.
- ❏ Write a first draft of the introduction to your paper.
- ❏ Explain what led to your interest in the topic and how you derived your research question.
- ❏ Work with peer reviewers, your cooperating teacher, and your university supervisor to gain feedback and constructive suggestions regarding the introduction of your paper.
- ❏ Glean input to your draft of the introduction and make the appropriate revisions.
- ❏ Polish your introduction and make sure it is descriptive, highly interesting, and will "hook" the reader.

*Identifying Best Practices*

In addition to meeting with your supervising teacher and discussing your thoughts and ideas with your college supervisor, professors, and other colleagues, you must turn to professional literature to help you gain access to best possible practices for your research study.

You will use your literature review to bring together or synthesize themes or commonalities found in similar research studies. A thorough review of the literature related to your research question may open up new ways of looking at the problem that might have been overlooked otherwise. It is also useful to see where studies appear to contradict each other. This may show you gaps in the research your study may help to answer. The literature review should not be a summary of what each journal article is about or an annotated bibliography. It should be a well-woven review of pertinent professional journal articles that you read in your topic area.

While it may be easy to summarize articles, a way to avoid this is to create an outline of what you found from your review of the literature before you begin writing. By having a common subject, topic, theme, or key area addressed by several studies, your thoughts will be better organized. Your study will become more focused once you see other investigators' examples of research questions, classroom research strategies, data collection procedures, and data analysis methods. In brief, reviewing other studies allows you to make the connection between theory and your own classroom practice.

When applicable, cite direct quotes from what you read in your research but be sure to justify why it is important enough to be shared. A common writing mistake is to insert one quote after another in a paper without a personal narrative of thoughts and inferences regarding the text. Doing this appropriately is actually connecting the dots for the reader. You are identifying important considerations pertaining to your personal question and topic. Be sure to be clear and concise!

At the conclusion of the literature review, include a paragraph that explains how what you have described will impact the question you are asking or how it will be important to your study. The following are some guidelines for writing your literature review.

1. Be clear in your thinking by knowing what you are doing in your classroom study.
2. Plan and organize your research well.
3. Emphasize connections between the information in the articles or books to the question of your study to ensure relevancy.
4. Properly credit the authors whose research results and ideas you discuss.
5. Summarize what you read in terms of the research question.
6. Expect to write multiple drafts of your literature review as you continuously proofread with a critical eye.
7. Seek feedback on your literature review by sharing and discussing it with others who are interested in your study.

*Getting Started with Your Literature Review*

1. Determine the keywords in your research question.
   Sample Question: Does the implementation of the Accelerated Reader software program improve reading comprehension?
   *Keywords:* Accelerated Reader, reading, comprehension
2. Think of some synonyms, related terms, or broader categories.
   Examples: computer-assisted instruction, rewards, motivation, understanding, reading improvement, effectiveness

*Where to Search*

1. All libraries' Web pages provide access to journal article databases for education such as www.sru.edu/library. (Note: Some of these databases are free to the public.)

2. MUST SEARCH: ERIC, Education Abstracts, Professional Development Collection in EBSCO databases.
3. OPTIONAL: Databases like Genderwatch and PsycINFO that might relate to your topic.
4. Google Scholar: scholar.google.com. You can locate scholarly articles but not usually in full text. Search library databases or use interlibrary loan to acquire full-text articles.

*How to Search*

1. Check scholarly and/or peer reviewed in Search options.
2. Use "and" to join single keywords, phrases. Words next to each other are interpreted as phrases. Example: Accelerated Reader and reading and comprehension
3. If articles are not available in full text, use interlibrary loan to request them for free. Most universities have a hot link for this on their library Web site.
4. To keep track of your articles, e-mail them to yourself. You can also separately e-mail citations in APA format from EBSCO databases.

*How to Cite*

1. Visit the online writing lab from Purdue University, owl.english.purdue.edu/.
2. Consult the APA manual (on reserve at most college libraries).

*How to Get Help*

Contact your campus education librarian. You will be pleasantly surprised how eager he/she will be to help you.

*How to Succeed*

1. Start early in case you need to get interlibrary loans from other universities.
2. Do not fall in love with your search terms. Try different words and phrases and different ways of approaching the topic.
3. Stand on the shoulders of giants. When you find a good article, look at its bibliography and literature review. Use the bibliography at the end of your articles to find further references.

It is important to remember that the library is an essential tool for developing your action research topic. Utilizing Internet resources properly is also a critical component to laying the foundation for your investigation.

The following is an example of how literature can be used to shape your practice.

## Exemplary Sample of Student Work: Site Words

### Literature Review

*Learning to read is essential in life. When children begin to learn to read they will encounter high frequency words or sight words. A sight word is a word known by sight and the word's identity is triggered in memory very rapidly (Ehri 2005). These words make up a significant portion of words in print.*

*It is important for children to learn these words. According to Phonics From A to Z (Blevins 1998), there are more than 600,000 words in the English language. Twenty-five percent of the words children read are the same thirteen words including a, and, for, he, is, in, it, of, that, the, to, was, you. These words carry little meaning but contribute to the flow of text (Novelli 2005). Ehri (2005) correlates the knowledge of the alphabet and sounds of the letters to the number of words a student can retain.*

*If a student knows the alphabet and sounds, Ehri suggests there is a positive correlation between the alphabet and the number of sight words retained. It is necessary for children to learn to read sight words because this will affect their reading and reading fluency in the future (Novelli 2005).*

*One way to remember sight words that can be practiced without the help of the teacher is by using flashcards, which promotes the drill and repetition method. Heinze (2006) suggests letting the children make their own flash-cards. Heinze points out that constructing the flashcards themselves promotes drill and repetition without the students knowing it.*

*One of the most effective ways to teach something new, such as sight words, is through use of the drill and repetition method. Burns and Dean (2005) found that having students drill and repeat new information showed an increase in the amount of sight words retained. My goal is to examine how drill and repetition activities can affect the retention of sight words.*

*—Laurel Beachem*

Remember, a good review of the literature should highlight themes, similarities, and differences between studies, not simply summarize an author's work.

### Checklist for Success
❑ Utilize academic journals produced by educational organizations and that are peer reviewed.
❑ Use caution with Internet searches such as Wikipedia. The information often lacks credibility. Books may be used, but make sure they are not outdated, lack credibility, or are too detailed.

❑ Examine the sample literature reviews that are included in this chapter.

❑ Generate an outline or web of the common themes or ideas you found in prior research that are related to your research topic before writing the narrative of your literature review.

❑ Check to see if the introduction and literature review align well together.

❑ Remember that findings for each article reviewed should be integrated (synthesized). If your paragraphs are a recap of each study, then you have not completed your review correctly.

❑ Skim to check if various studies (copyright dates from APA format) are included throughout the review. Be sure to add each cited study to your reference section.

❑ Receive peer, cooperating teacher, and university supervisor feedback.

❑ Based on that input, implement appropriate revisions to the literature review.

❑ Complete the final draft of the literature review.

*Developing Research Methods*

Quite simply, the methodology section should be written as if it were a recipe. It does not need to be lengthy, but it does need to be specific enough that anyone without previous cooking abilities could follow it in order to have a successful outcome. This is the goal you should keep in mind as you write your description of what data you will collect, when you will collect it, from what sources you will collect it, and how you intend to analyze it.

Consider the artifacts, tools, or sources that will help you find answers and insights regarding your research question. Garner a variety of possible data sources. When possible, organize many of these sources according to your research goals. The following is a brief list of possible data sources (Johnson 2003; Sagor 1992):

- individual student tests or quizzes
- student interviews (audio tapes)
- student writing samples
- student homework
- student attendance records
- student journals
- small group conferences
- teacher journals/logs
- teacher field notes
- teacher interviews
- classroom observations

- lesson plans
- student or teacher checklists
- videotapes of class activities
- student surveys/attitude/rating scales
- graphic organizers
- student projects, artwork, or performance assessments

It is also beneficial to keep a data log (or record in a separate section of your teacher-as-researcher journal) to indicate *when* all information is collected, the *time*, the *place*, and the *data itself*. As you consider the types of data you plan to collect, think about how you might triangulate the data to help you make reasonable inferences. You should try to triangulate at least three different sources of information so you can determine if they corroborate. It will bolster the credibility of your final conclusions.

Consider the following example of why you should triangulate. You may interview several students regarding their opinion of how social studies is taught in their classroom. The conclusion you may draw is that they dislike social studies. Basing your inference on the interviews alone could be flawed because the students may be trying to influence what happens in their classrooms. Perhaps they believe that by saying that they do not like social studies they might gain more recess time or have the teacher fired. However, if you also interview the teacher and the teacher concurs that the students seem bored and inattentive during class, you will have two valid points of comparison.

If you analyze student test scores and see that the class average is very poor in social studies, you now have three sources of evidence all pointing to the same conclusion. This triangulation makes your statements and conclusions credible.

Note that triangulation does not have to include three completely different sources. Student interviews, your own anecdotal notes written during observations of social studies lessons, accompanied by a questionnaire of what students do not like about social studies class would constitute triangulation. This holds true even though the data is all collected from the same students. There are three primary benefits of triangulation: It allows for imperfections or flaws in one of the data sources or collection instruments; it increases confidence in the results when all three sources corroborate; and it assists in the development of important questions or insights when sources do not support the same results (Sagor 1992).

There is one cautionary note about conducting student interviews. Be sure that you check with the school regarding appropriate parental permission procedures if you choose to interview them at points in the day that are not part of regular classroom instruction. This becomes more important if you plan to audiotape (a preferred method for interviews) or videotape.

Recording your work allows more time to analyze the responses and perhaps to transcribe them onto paper for analysis. It is important to also develop what is coined a *protocol*. This is a set of questions (or prompts) that you intend to ask in the interviews.

Another feature to consider while in the planning stage of your research is whether your data-collection methods will be valid. In other words, consider what you plan to collect and then align your artifacts with your question. Will the artifacts aid you in answering your research question? This may sound rather obvious, but when you are ensconced in the details of data-gathering procedures, it is easy to stray off course. You may later come to the unfortunate realization in the data analysis that what you have collected really will not help you make valid conclusions about your research question.

Another consideration is reliability. The difference between reliability and validity is that reliability is the accuracy of your measurement or assessment and validity is whether it measures what you want it to measure. One way to check the reliability and validity of your study is to pretend you are a reader looking at your study results for the first time. Will the reader be convinced that the information you collected or measured is consistently accurate?

An essential aspect of your methodology should be the data collection timeline. In order to gather the data needed for the study, it is important that you schedule what and when collection will occur. Plotting this on the school calendar will help you accomplish your goals. Planning is everything during a short window of opportunity!

Finally, the methodology section of your paper must include methods regarding maintenance of the confidentiality of research data. Student names should be removed from collected work samples and kept confidential. Only data without names can be reported in your paper. Responses should be collected without any identification so you will have student anonymity and the work remains anonymous because not even the researcher is able to tell who submitted which samples. If individual student's work needs to be analyzed and displayed, identify each student as Student 1, Student 2, and so on so that student confidentiality is not compromised.

Exemplary Sample of Student Work:
Using Manipulatives to Teach Fractions

*Methodology*

*This study is being conducted in a classroom of eighteen third-grade students ranging in age from eight to nine years old. At the beginning of the study of fractions, a pre-test will be given to the entire class. Based on the results of this pre-test, I will identify students who appear to be at-risk and struggling with the concept of fractions.*

*I will take these students and, over the course of two weeks, teach them four lessons during small-group time in math lab. The lessons will be concentrated on using a highly manipulative-based, hands-on lesson that in most cases goes beyond what a classroom teacher can do when focusing on more students and the demands of an entire classroom.*

*Lesson 1 will focus on identifying the numerator and denominator of a fraction and defining a fraction. I will stress that a fraction must always have equal parts. We will then practice dividing different shapes into equal parts. They will have to choose or shade a certain number of parts. From the shape, the students will have to then write the correct fraction that is represented from the shaded portion. We will work with both written shapes on paper and with circle fraction manipulatives to show a representation of the given parts.*

*Lesson 2 is based around fractions as part of a group. Using manipulative counters, I will have the students count out a certain number of "bears" to form their set. I then will ask them to divide the set into a number of equal parts. I will demonstrate counting one bear into each set and continue giving each group one additional bear until my set is dispersed. We then will talk about whether the groups are equal, and if this could be a representation of a fraction, going back to the definition of fractions (equal parts).*

*In lesson 3, we will continue with fractions as part of a set or group and work with both manipulatives and on paper to divide sets into equal parts. I then will take the concept a step further and begin to ask the students, "What is one-fourth of this set of twelve?"*

*In lesson 4, we will again review and reinforce the concept of fractions using a variety of manipulatives to reinforce the concepts we are trying to solidify. Again, the lessons will be focused on showing, and not just telling, the students about fractions. This is a mixed review of all the skills and concepts that will be covered during our lessons, and I will concentrate on transferring the manipulative-based understandings to written work.*

*I will collect the data from the four lessons and again give the students the same test as I will at the beginning of the unit. This will be to assess whether the increased use of manipulatives and study with a small group of students will impact the scores on the test.*

*—Vickie Waugaman*

Your methodology section should fully describe the sequence and methods of the study for the purpose of deriving the answers to your research question.

### Checklist for Success
❏ Review the exemplary methodology samples in this chapter.
❏ Locate preexisting data collection tools that will aid you in learning about this topic.

❏ Identify different sources of data that will best allow you to investigate the topic.

❏ Estimate how much data you will need to collect in order to study this topic.

❏ Consider the ways in which you can build data collection and recording into normal classroom activities (e.g., observations, tests).

❏ Align the introduction, literature review and methodology with the research question.

❏ Ascertain that there is a match between what you hope to learn from the study and the data-collection methods you will use.

❏ Develop a comprehensive plan for data collection including a timeline.

❏ Discuss your data-collection methodology with peer reviewers, your cooperating teacher, and the university supervisor to gain feedback and constructive criticism regarding your ideas for procedures and sources.

❏ Finalize the process for data collection.

❏ Prepare a clear narrative describing the data-collection process.

❏ Share the methodology section of your paper with peer reviewers, your cooperating teacher, and your university supervisor to gain feedback and constructive criticism.

### Step 4: Plan Activation (Following through with Your Methodology)

The next phase is to implement your methodology, while being aware that some modification and changes may be necessary. Unforeseen factors may require you to reflect upon how well your initial plan is working. This may lead to minor changes or adaptations, which is expected during action research. Making such changes embodies the true spirit of a reflection-in-action practitioner, described in chapter 1, and allows and encourages you to make changes as a response to what the data reveal about your current work with your children.

### Step 5: Outcome Assessment

The primary objective of your outcome assessment is to measure the effectiveness of your actions based on data. You can use this information to draw some conclusions and improve your own teaching and possibly the teaching of others by realizing the implications. Finally, you can make some recommendations related to your inquiry.

*What Is the Data Telling You?*

Your data analysis should be meaningful. In order to accomplish this you must:

- Record observations systematically, carefully, and precisely
- Describe exactly what you did during the data collection and throughout the analysis
- Record and report everything of importance
- Describe and interpret your data objectively
- Use data sources that can answer your questions
- Look at your data from multiple angles/perspectives

Sagor (1992) also provides two insightful questions to ask when analyzing your data:

1. What are the important themes observed that will help answer your research question?
2. How much of your data supports each of the themes?

To answer these questions, you now have to decide how you will separate your data to examine the themes that may have surfaced. Some common methods for data analysis include organizing your data into piles and using sticky notes or highlighters (manual or word processing) to code important snippets of information.

You may also want to organize your data into tables, graphs, matrices, charts, or graphic organizers. Write down themes, patterns, and larger concepts that emerge in the data you have collected. Sort information into themes and then minimize your list to one with a few themes. (The sample data analysis at the end of this section demonstrates themes identified regarding multiplication facts.) Take notes as you proceed and review your data to locate points that occur more frequently and seem most powerful. Now, write down your major points and match the data you collected with each major point.

Since every research project is unique, there is no one single approach that is best for each study. The chart in figure 3.3 may assist you by providing a guide sheet for data analysis. You must become immersed in your information in order to deduce important findings and results. You will know you have looked at your data deeply enough when you begin to feel like you are looking at the same answers, scores, or responses over and over again until you feel like you almost have them memorized.

Exemplary Sample of Student Work:
Interactive Learning Methods

*Data Analysis*

*The data in this study has shown how students can make significant advancements in mathematics skill level when provided with interactive learning*

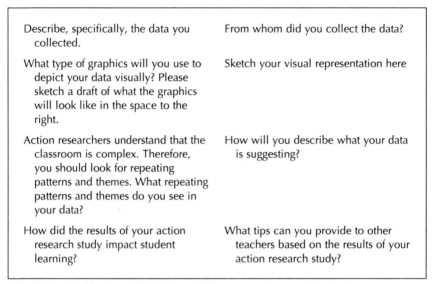

| | |
|---|---|
| Describe, specifically, the data you collected. | From whom did you collect the data? |
| What type of graphics will you use to depict your data visually? Please sketch a draft of what the graphics will look like in the space to the right. | Sketch your visual representation here |
| Action researchers understand that the classroom is complex. Therefore, you should look for repeating patterns and themes. What repeating patterns and themes do you see in your data? | How will you describe what your data is suggesting? |
| How did the results of your action research study impact student learning? | What tips can you provide to other teachers based on the results of your action research study? |

**Figure 3.3.   Guide Sheet for Data Analysis**

*methods. Specifically, this study has shown the differential achievement of students with and without learning disabilities, in multiplication fact recall, over a four-week period.*

*Data was collected from five, one-minute, 100-problem multiplication tests. The same test was administered to all students during five testing sessions. Between each testing session, all students played one of four multiplication games including a dice game, a multiplication ball game, a number tile game, and a card game. All students played the same game during the same week.*

*After the four-week study period, I compiled the students' test results into a chart that visually represents student achievement. The data in this chart shows the percent increase in individual group achievement based on the study week and the game played. The percent increase was determined for both students with and without learning disabilities based on average scores from both groups. Individual student scores were first averaged for each week throughout the study. Then the average scores were used to reflect percent increase between the baseline scores and the individual weeks. The data was plugged into the following formula: Week – Baseline / Baseline 100. This determined the weekly percent increase of problems completed and problems correct for each group.*

*The bar graph (figure 3.4) shows the weekly percent increase for both students with learning disabilities and students without. This data shows that while each week student skill level increased from the baseline, the increase was determined by the game that was played. The data shows that each*

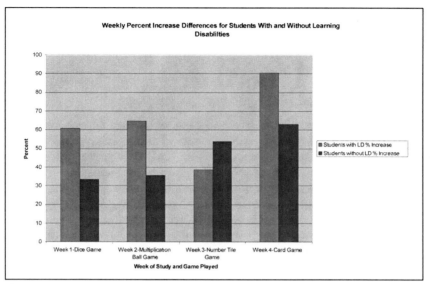

**Figure 3.4.  Exemplary Student Data**

*group made significant increases in multiplication recall ability throughout the study.*

*The data (figure 3.4) show that both students with and without learning disabilities can increase multiplication fact recall ability through the use of math games. The data show that while both groups made substantial gains, it was the students with learning disabilities that had the most improvement over the four-week period.*

*—Dana Pears*

### Checklist for Success

❑ Study the exemplary data analysis samples included in this chapter.

❑ Discuss the qualities of accurate and credible data analysis with your cooperating teacher and university supervisor.

❑ Discuss the procedures for conducting a thorough data analysis with your cooperating teacher and university supervisor.

❑ Generate and draft a comprehensive plan for your data analysis.

❑ Finalize an effective plan for analyzing your research data.

❑ Complete a polished draft of your data analysis.

❑ Share your data analysis with peer reviewers, your cooperating teacher, and your university supervisor to gain feedback and constructive criticism.

❑ Collaborate with peer reviewers, your cooperating teacher, and your university supervisor and get feedback and constructive criticism

regarding the alignment of your introduction, literature review, methodology, and data analysis.
❑ Write and polish appropriate revisions to your data analysis based on their input.

*What Conclusions Can You Draw Based Upon the Data?*

Now is the time to report what you have found through your study and to draw conclusions. Remember, the *process* of doing your research is as significant as the findings in your study. You should have grown in confidence that you have the tools to solve future classroom problems.

In order to authentically report the results in your study, you need to keep in mind that your audience will not have personal knowledge of your data. Therefore, you have to find a simplistic, reader-friendly way to share the facts that answer or provide insight into your research question. This is commonly done through graphs, tables, charts, or narratives that may be supported by student quotes. When writing the conclusion of your study, do not use the word *proves*. Remember that your research is not going to "prove" anything, but rather it is going to help you "improve" your own teaching. A better choice would be *suggests, may indicate,* or that the results of your study *show promise* regarding the topic.

It will be helpful to look back at your literature review and see how your study conclusions compare to the other studies you analyzed before you began your topic. Deep connections and valuable reflection occur by linking your own findings to what other researchers have discovered about the topic. Drawing conclusions about your work and review of the literature also strengthens your credibility when you make recommendations for your plan of action and for other teachers interested in your topic.

Remember that having results that did not meet your expectations does not constitute failure! It simply tells you that the technique or problem as analyzed is not an ideal route and that changes would be needed if the study were to be repeated. Bottom line: Your action research study conclusions do not have to change the world! It is acceptable to write that your results were not what you had expected. Research that finds what *doesn't* work is just as important as research that finds what *does* work. Gaining insight into why study results were not optimal is what is most important. Acting on what has been learned is a vital component of action research.

Once you have written the facts and results you discovered in your study, the conclusion to your paper is merely a description of what you know to be true based on the data you collected. Be sure to reflect and share your personal insights when writing study results in the conclusion of your paper. Report on what the students learned and what you learned about teaching. What strengths and weaknesses are you able to conclude about your research?

In sum, you are writing a story about how you investigated the facts you included in your study and why you feel they are relevant to your question. Emphasize the logical connections you are able to determine from your study. These connections may not become obvious to your readers simply by looking at the visuals of the study. This is the point where everything comes together. It is essential that you relate your study conclusions back to your research question. Did your findings answer your research question in full or do the results leave you with only partial answers and many other new questions? How do your results differ from what you thought you would learn? It must be emphasized that it is vital to divulge this important component of your study with the reading audience. It helps bring your action research full circle, from the question to the answer. Making connections as a reflective practitioner is key to growing as a professional.

When you write your conclusion, consider it as a post-project reflection. In other words, what did you learn from the project? Do this by reflecting about the following topics:

- teaching in general
- teaching in the targeted academic area
- your students
- your teaching style and procedures
- your assessment strategies

Most important, what impact did you have on the students' learning in the targeted area? How do you know? Support your answers with assessment data and with your observations. Use appropriate terminology and demonstrate your understanding of student development.

### Exemplary Sample of Student Work: Interactive Learning

#### Conclusion

*The data from the weekly assessments shows that the students with learning disabilities made the greatest gains in multiplication fact recall through the use of math games. The figure shows that each group made considerable gains, but in the end it was the students with learning disabilities that made the most significant gains based on baseline and weekly testing scores.*

*The results show that in a differential study using multiplication games to enhance fact recall ability, students with disabilities show a higher level of achievement than students without learning disabilities. The results show that both groups made advancements; however, the improvements of the students with learning disabilities were more significant. From the baseline to the end of the fourth week, students with learning disabilities showed a 91 percent increase in the number of problems correctly completed compared to a 63 percent increase for students without learning disabilities.*

*I believe that students with and without learning disabilities could have continued to make gains in multiplication fact recall ability if the games were continually used. I believe that the students with learning disabilities would continue to show the greatest increase in achievement based on the premise that the games meet their specific learning styles.*

*—Dana Pears*

Keep in mind that, in general, your audience will not have personal knowledge of your data. Be sure you have a simplistic, reader-friendly approach to share the facts that answer or provide insight into your research question.

**Checklist for Success**
- ❏ Examine the Exemplary Conclusion samples included in this chapter and note the accompanying figures, graphs, charts, tables that enhance reader understanding.
- ❏ Outline a framework for your data presentation (charts, graphs, narrative, etc.) and design descriptive statistics and graphs or tables to clearly illustrate the results of your research.
- ❏ Draft an outline of key points for the narrative results and conclusions section.
- ❏ Obtain peer, cooperating teacher, and university supervisor feedback on the narrative draft and the visuals of the conclusions section of your study.
- ❏ Polish and revise the conclusions narrative and visuals of your paper based on the feedback and suggestions you gleaned from your peers, cooperating teacher, and university supervisor.
- ❏ Collaborate with peer reviewers, your cooperating teacher, and your university supervisor and get feedback and constructive criticism regarding the alignment of your introduction, literature review, methodology, data analysis, and conclusions.
- ❏ http://nces.ed.gov/nceskids/createagraph/default.aspx is a great graphing Web site to use if you are new to graph construction!

*Implications and Recommendations*

Action research is one avenue for bringing teachers together to share their concerns and figure out a way to find answers for them. Doing this is quite important, but it is often the most neglected part of the action research process. Bear in mind that this project is called *action* research, so this is where you explain what actions did or did not work in the classroom and what actions you now will try or recommend. Provide specific details in your recommendations so that others can easily implement them in their own classrooms.

What actions might you take based on the study results? You are to develop a plan of action, which is a description of your intentions or a list of steps you plan to take to improve your classroom practice in the topic under study.

Your plan may result in one of five outcomes: a greater understanding of the topic or problem, the discovery of a new or underlying problem, a plan or method that may be effective in the classroom, a plan or method that may need to be revised or modified, or a plan or method that may be ineffective in the classroom. The bottom line is that action research is a mechanism for professional growth for teachers who are willing to devote the necessary time and energy to it. It is an excellent way to link personal professional growth with school change aimed at improved student learning.

## Exemplary Sample of Student Work: Interactive Learning

### *Implications*

*According to this study, the results show that implementing instructional games in the classroom will help students recall their sight words. It is a fun and easy way for teachers to bring sight word practice into their own classroom. I have found that the kindergarten students enjoyed getting to get up to play games, instead of always writing the words or practicing the words using flash cards. I believe that any age group of students love getting a chance to get up and move around. It's a great way to incorporate movement into the day.*

*Teachers need to remember how important sight word knowledge is to the reading process. Sight words are part of the basis of learning to read. Many sight words are words that are not able to be sounded out. Therefore these words need to be accessed into the student's memory. If students master a lot of sight words then they will be able to read more fluently. This strategy helps students enjoy reading more and reading can be a lot less stressful.*

*It is very simple for a teacher to integrate these easy games into the school day. Many of them are simple enough; they can be added when there is a little bit of down time. Another great time to use these games is when the students are working in centers or small groups. A teacher could even ask a parent volunteer to run one of these games in a center.*

*I believe that the use of these games can be helpful in any age classroom. I would strongly recommend that teachers use these games to aid students in their acquisition of sight words. I have found that reviewing these words only two or three times a week helped these students learn their sight words more rapidly. This study has shown the importance of reviewing sight words with students and how repetition can help students learn faster.*

*—Erin Williams*

One of the benefits of doing action research is that your findings can be used to enlighten other teachers. Your ability to share specific implications and recommendations may be of great assistance to other teachers.

### Checklist for Success
❏ Analyze the "Implications for Other Teachers" examples that are included in this chapter.
❏ Develop a plan for improved classroom instruction based upon a review of your completed study.
❏ Draft the narrative describing the plan for improved instruction.
❏ Implement the plan for improved instruction and collect post-implementation data.
❏ Draft an outline of key points for the implications section before writing the narrative.
❏ Obtain peer, cooperating teacher, and university supervisor feedback on the narrative draft of the implications section of your study.
❏ Polish and revise the implications and plan for improved instruction narrative of your paper based on the feedback and suggestions you gained from your peers, cooperating teacher, and university supervisor.
❏ Collaborate with peer reviewers, your cooperating teacher, and your university supervisor and get feedback and constructive criticism regarding the alignment of your introduction, literature review, methodology, data analysis, conclusions, and implications.

## REFERENCES: CRAFTING YOUR REFERENCE LIST AND USING THE AMERICAN PSYCHOLOGICAL ASSOCIATION (APA) STYLE FORMAT

Once they complete their papers, many students mistakenly believe they are finished! It is vital to ensure that you have included and properly cited each resource you utilized in your work. The sources displayed in figure 3.5 will help you ensure you are citing your references properly.

In essence, properly citing your scholarly references is crucial to gaining professional credibility for your research. Therefore, it is imperative that you include and properly cite each resource you utilized in your work.

**HOW TO CITE IT: APA Style For Education**

| | |
|---|---|
| APA Style Manual | Available at library reference and circulation desks |
| APA Web Site | www.apastyle.org/ |
| Citation Machine | citationmachine.net |
| OWL at Purdue University | owl.english.purdue.edu/owl/resource/560/01/ |

**Figure 3.5. How to Cite APA**
Note: Contents of figure 3.5 graciously provided by Melba Tomeo, Slippery Rock Librarian.

### Checklist for Success

❑ Study the preceding APA guide sheet both before and after writing your action research paper.

❑ Double-check your references and citations to ensure that they are written in proper APA format.

❑ Consult the APA manual, university librarians, or your supervisor if you have any questions.

❑ Find each parenthesized date from your cited work (the APA format) in the body of your work. As you do, check it off in the reference list. This will allow you to ensure that each reference was included and also allows you to spot any citations you may have originally included as a reference but later removed in the final draft.

❑ Compile all of the sections of the research paper as a nearly finished draft.

❑ Critique final drafts of peer action research papers in pairs or in small groups.

❑ Polish and revise your completed action research paper based on the feedback and suggestions you obtained from your peers, cooperating teacher, and university supervisor.

❑ Collaborate with peer reviewers, your cooperating teacher, and your university supervisor and get feedback and constructive criticism regarding the alignment of your introduction, literature review, methodology, data analysis, conclusions, implications, and references.

❑ Complete final revisions or modifications of the action research paper.

## SHARING YOUR ACTION RESEARCH WITH OTHERS

Now that you have completed your planned methodology, collected and analyzed the data, and formulated some ideas on how to improve or change your own teaching in the future, it is time to share your hard work

| CATEGORY | Developing | At Standard | Advanced |
|---|---|---|---|
| **Introduction** | Lacks detailed discussion of the setting and or reasons for selecting the research question. | Describes the setting and reasons for selecting the research question adequately. | Thoroughly explains the setting and characteristics of the school/students, the reasoning that led to the selection of the question, why the question is important, and how the study helped provide insight into candidate's teaching. |
| **Literature Review** | The literature review is a list of study summaries and/or uses less than five professional sources | The literature review is described clearly, but lacks integration of the sources or does not utilize at least five professional sources. | Describes and synthesizes the content with relevant topics and adequately uses five professional sources. Clearly connects the professional literature reviewed to the research question. |
| **Methodology** | The procedures followed are vague and lack specific detail. | The methodology was explained clearly, but lacks enough detail for others to follow if repeating the study. | Sufficient information is presented in a clear and concise manner to explain the step-by-step procedure of what was done in the study and how the study was implemented and measured. |

| | | | |
|---|---|---|---|
| **Data Analysis** | The data analysis lacks clarity and objective interpretation. | Adequately describes how the data was collected and interpreted. | Describes clearly what was done during the data collection and analysis. Evidence that the data was interpreted objectively from multiple angles/perspectives exists. |
| **Conclusions** | The results and conclusions lack clarity and contain inadequate representation of the data. | Results are clearly described and the data included supports the conclusions. | Includes assessment data and a clear reflection of how the effectiveness was assessed. Communicates results clearly and includes figures, graphs/charts that support the findings. |
| **Implications** | Discusses implications in a general manner or provides suggestions that are not closely related to the results of the study. | Describes the implications drawn from the study; suggests general instructional practices or strategies for fellow educators to implement. | Describes the implications drawn from the study and suggests specific instructional practices or strategies for fellow educators to implement. Suggestions are clearly related to the results. |

**Figure 3.6.   Self-Evaluation (Rubric) of Your Written Paper or PowerPoint**

and valuable insight! All of your efforts should not go unnoticed by others in the field, so consider the best way for you to disseminate your work.

This is the culmination of your action research project. Now you are ready to share your action research study with colleagues or university faculty. You will want to do so in an efficient and professional manner. You may choose to display your action research via a trifold poster, a written paper, or a PowerPoint presentation.

If presenting via a poster board, all text on your display should be typed material unless handwritten items strengthen or support your presentation topic. A sample is shown in figure 3.7.

### Tips for Creating an Effective Poster Board

1. Have items mounted with inconspicuous materials, such as staples or double-sided or rolled tape. The use of tacks and duct tape should be avoided.
2. Avoid the use of multicolored patterns. Remember that this is not a bulletin board for a first grade classroom but a professional display to share with peers and colleagues. The use of colored poster board or color added to titles or background mats for white text or graphics are recommended as formats.
3. Refrain from making the poster look too busy or cluttered.
4. Type your research title or question at the top of your poster and center it. (Be sure to include a question mark if your title is a question.)
5. The poster title should be of a font size that fits neatly in one or two lines across the top of the poster and should be noticeably larger than the section subtitles.
6. Items attached that are cut smaller than an 8 1/2 x 11 sheet of paper, such as the title and name, should be cut with a paper cutter or scoring knife rather than scissors.
7. Sections with multiple pages should be stapled together and included for each of the required poster subtitles.
8. When possible, visual aids such as concept maps, charts, diagrams, or graphs should be the primary emphasis for your display. The poster should portray a clear understanding of your study to the audience. Visual aids often make it easier to convey your research.

If communicating your study results as a written paper or PowerPoint instead of a poster session, a rubric, as shown in figure 3.6, can assist you in organizing and self-assessing your paper. Your cooperating teacher or supervisor may also utilize the rubric in figure 3.6 to provide feedback on your work.

In this section, we have emphasized a poster-presentation format. Remember that you may also choose to utilize another format such as a Pow-

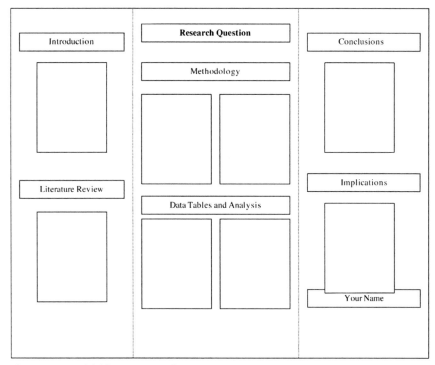

**Figure 3.7.  Tri-fold Poster Sample Layout**

erPoint presentation, which can easily be developed to follow the written paper format.

### Checklist for Success
- ❏ Obtain peer feedback on your tri-fold presentation board and visuals, especially regarding your data collection and data analysis.
- ❏ Review the exemplary action research report presentation boards that your university supervisor may share with you.
- ❏ Label and attach artifacts and paper sections to your poster so they are fastened securely.
- ❏ Prepare the research presentation tri-fold using the tri-fold layout sheet.
- ❏ Develop strategies for presenting the report.

## QUESTIONS FOR REVIEW AND REFLECTION

1. What elements define a well-designed research question?
2. What types of sources should you use when researching a topic?

3. Why is it important to ensure that the review of the literature is organized by themes and includes an integration of the studies?
4. What is the purpose of a methodology section for conducting research?
5. What are three ways to display the results after analyzing your data?
6. What is the most important consideration to determine whether you have arrived at an accurate conclusion based on the data collected?
7. Why is it important to offer specific recommendations for other teachers?
8. What are three possible outcomes of your action research?
9. Describe two ways that you can professionally share what you have learned from your research findings.

## REFERENCES

Hubbard, R. & Powell, B. (1999). *Living the questions: A guide for teacher researchers.* Portland, ME: Stenhouse Publishers.

Johnson, A. P. (2003). *What every teacher should know about action research.* Boston: Allyn & Bacon-Pearson Education.

Sagor, R. (1992). *How to conduct collaborative action research.* Alexandria, VA: Association for Supervision and Curriculum Development.

# II

## A CROSS SECTION OF ACTION RESEARCH APPLICATIONS

# 4

## Action Research and the Early Childhood Educator

*Linda Taylor, EdD, Assistant Professor of Education, Ball State University, Indiana*

*Susan H. Pillets, M.S., Kindergarten Teacher, Baltimore County Public Schools, Maryland*

### INTRODUCTION

A child's early years are typically spent in a variety of settings such as family homes, daycare centers, nursery schools, Head Start programs, prekindergarten programs, and traditional classrooms for kindergarten through third grade. There is a whole host of basic skills that children need to acquire within accepted timeframes, and learning therefore must be facilitated by family, friends, educators, and acquaintances who interact with each child.

This chapter will explore how you can effectively implement action research in any early childhood setting, in order to ensure that every child reaches their maximum potential, in psychosocial as well academic contexts. The following pages will assist you in refining your personal reflections into appropriate action, by learning the mindset and applying the skill sets of an early childhood action researcher.

## CHAPTER OBJECTIVES

By the time you finish reading and thinking about this chapter, you will be able to:

- Recognize the benefits of action research in any early childhood setting.
- Identify and address special considerations when conducting action research in early childhood settings and recognize how it may look different than in elementary or secondary programs.
- Identify potential action research topics such as school readiness questions in early childhood settings.

## THE SCHOOL READINESS QUESTION EXPLAINED

The National Association for the Education of Young Children (NAEYC) defines early childhood as the years from birth through age eight, which are the years when major cognitive and physical development takes place.

If you are pursuing a degree in Early Childhood Education, you may have already encountered a common misperception that you will primarily be a caretaker or babysitter and not necessarily need the type the education of a "real" teacher. Central to that misconception is that in order to be a successful educator in an early childhood setting, you simply need a love of children.

As educators, we know the above statements are far from the truth. More accurately, the first eight years of a child's life typically provides the foundation for all future learning. It can not be understated, therefore, that we must work harder than ever to build a solid and secure foundation in the early childhood years, to make successful the experiences of all future learning.

With the increased focus on school readiness in the past few years, action research in early childhood settings has taken root. In Maryland, for example, beginning in 2001, the State Department of Education began conducting an ongoing action research project, the Maryland Model for School Readiness (MMSR). The MMSR is designed to determine the correlation between prior school experience and school readiness of students entering kindergarten in Maryland public schools.

Few states have a formal definition for school readiness other than an age requirement for eligibility (Saluja Scott-Little, & Clifford 2000); however, the Maryland State Department of Education defines school readiness as:

the state of early development that enables an individual child to engage in and benefit from early learning experiences. As a result of family nurturing and interactions with others, a young child in this stage has reached certain levels of social and emotional development, cognition and general knowledge, language development, and physical well-being and motor development. School readiness acknowledges individual approaches toward learning as well as the unique experiences and backgrounds of each child.

In an action research project that spans more than eight years, kindergarten educators in Maryland have been documenting the prior school experiences of children and identifying their levels of proficiency on thirty different social, emotional, personal, and cognitive indicators. The Maryland Model for School Readiness has been used to request increased funding for prekindergarten programs and to establish a correlation between prior school experience and increased school readiness.

In light of the No Child Left Behind Act and the increased accountability for educators at every level, many primary teachers are beginning to use action research to examine the characteristics and skills children need to be ready for school. At every level, the early childhood student is so vastly different that it is important to understand what skills are prerequisite skills in order to master other skills. Keep in mind that young children are very influenced by those around them and that the development within any classroom spans a twelve-month time frame. Think about the newborn and the one-year-old child and the differences developmentally during those twelve months. Some of those developmental differences will be apparent in a classroom setting during the primary years and will impact when children master skills. An understanding of appropriate expectations for children when they enter formal schooling will guide your personal evaluation of the strategies you use to help children meet these expectations. You will see in the coming pages how such reflection is a valuable tool for early childhood action researchers.

## A HISTORY OF EARLY
## CHILDHOOD ACTION RESEARCHERS

In chapter 1, you read about the general evolution of action research and perhaps you are now questioning just how this process is conducted with two-year-olds or five-year-olds who are not able to read or explain what they are thinking. In reviewing the literature related to action research in the early childhood setting, it is apparent that the topic has gotten little attention when compared to action research being conducted with other groups.

Lilia Lasky (1978), one of the initial early childhood action researchers, drew attention to the need, efficacy, and appropriateness of using action research in the early childhood setting. She explored patterns in children's behaviors and matched teaching strategies to the needs of young children and her work set the tone for recent research that identifies the vast benefits for educators and preservice teachers conducting action research with their early childhood learners (Hatch, Greer, & Bailey 2006).

Conducting action research has become widely used by colleges and universities as a coursework requirement for preservice teachers and as a method for learning systematic inquiry to address issues or questions that arise in classroom settings. The benefits and uses of action research are well documented at every level of education from preschool to institutes of higher education.

## THE EARLY CHILDHOOD ACTION RESEARCH TEACHER

As a reflective practitioner, it is second nature to ask yourself what worked, what did not work, and what should be changed the next time you teach a lesson. Teachers find reflection a valuable tool as it informs their planning, which in turn sculpts their practices and results in increased student achievement. Although encouraging teacher reflection by questioning actions, planning for student interests, and examining teaching practices is the cornerstone of instruction at such places as the famed Diana School, in Reggio Emilia, we are now seeing these strategies more widely used elsewhere in early childhood education (Malaguzzi 1998).

You will find that early childhood action research is often an unfolding process; the teacher continuously reflects on what is occurring and alters plans based on continuous observations of children. In chapter 1, this is referred to as *responsive teaching*. Teacher observation then leads to new reflection, new issues for research, and additional observations or a continuous cycle of research and action.

Of greatest importance to the teacher-researcher are the questions that cannot be answered without investigation. For example, if you have one child who has difficulty participating in group settings, you may try a variety of actions to get him involved with other children. Through trial and error, you will be able to figure out what works with that child. However, if you consistently have the majority of children displaying difficult behavior during group times, you may want to set up a systematic method of trying different strategies when conducting group times. This is perfect opportunity for the application of early childhood action research.

## REFLECTION IN ACTION—FIVE CASE STUDIES

Reflective early childhood teachers who examine what works in their classrooms are already doing action research, albeit informally. As a teacher candidate who practices reflection in action, you will soon see how a more formal research approach benefits both you and your students.

Research indicates that preservice teachers who conduct action research become more thoughtful about their teaching strategies and gain confidence as teachers and problem solvers (Hatch, Greer, & Bailey 2006). The following action research projects arose from each teacher's reflection, issue identification, data collection, action planning, plan activation, and outcome assessment. They show how action research can be implemented in a variety of early childhood settings.

### Case 1: Mrs. Tweet's Five-Year-Olds

*A teacher of eighteen five-year-olds, Mrs. Tweet, described her class as very chatty and easily distracted by their peers. She knew the children did not listen well when she tried to conduct circle times with the whole class and thus when the children went to learning centers for the day, they could not remember what they were to do. In an effort to address this problem, the teacher explored the question, "What impact would assigned seats during circle time have on the children's listening comprehension?"*

*The teacher selected two children, a boy and a girl, who she felt were the least able to listen to instructions and follow directions. For one week prior to providing teacher-assigned seats for circle time and two weeks after the seating change was implemented, Mrs. Tweet checked to see if these children could remember the stated journal topic for the day once they arrived at the writing center to begin work on their journals.*

*While the baseline data showed the children were unable to remember the topic, the teacher found that assigning seats did improve the listening comprehension of the students. An added benefit to the assigned seats was that the whole class improved in their ability to focus, listen, and follow directions when they reached the learning centers.*

Mrs. Tweet first identified the issues of distraction and comprehension, collected data to validate the identified issues (which showed that the children were unable to recall the journal topic) and then planned an appropriate action of assigned seating to address the issues. She then implemented her plan of assigned seating, recorded the ability of the students to recall the journal topic, and then was able to show how the action impacted the issue.

As stated in chapter 1, the "action" of action research is the activities you do as a teaching professional in the classroom and the "research" is the methods of data collection, the professional habits of observation, the attitude of openly searching for new and better ways to present material and challenge your students, and the disposition to be a reflective practitioner. Based on Mrs. Tweet's action research, she decided to take a specific course of action and adapt her class's circle time to meet the needs of this group of children. The subsequent data she collected (research) demonstrated that reducing the amount of sit time effectively addressed the issues of distraction and comprehension. In her future circle times, children were chatty and more attentive.

## Case 2: Mrs. Jeffs's Motor Development Class

*A nursery school teacher of three- to five-year-olds observed that some children were unaware of the meaning of personal space and easily distracted during circle time. She wondered how to help the children regulate their personal space while she gave directions and warmed up for motor development activities.*

*Mrs. Jeffs decided that carpet squares and the defined area of a carpet square might help the children with the identified issues. After implementing the use of carpet squares during circle time, she began collecting information and discovered that the younger children required more direction to space themselves and pay attention while the older children needed less assistance in regulating their personal space.*

*Her results showed that approximately one-quarter of the three-year-old children in each class needed assistance managing their personal space while only 1 in 20 children needed assistance in the five-year-old class. Although the carpet squares gave consistency and predictability to a class, Mrs. Jeffs concluded that it was not a major component to a successful class. As a result of her findings, Mrs. Jeffs adjusted her plans for organizing the younger groups of children but made no changes for the older classes of children.*

Mrs. Jeffs answered her question about regulating personal space while engaging in the cyclical nature of action research discussed in chapter 1. Her results led to new questions about other components for creating a successful class session, which in turn led to further research and action. Mrs. Jeffs was able to accomplish all that with children who weren't accomplished at expressing their thoughts and ideas and were unable to read or write.

## Case 3: Ms. Galway's Parent Survey

*Ms. Galway, a daycare teacher of infants and toddlers, surveyed parents to find out if they wanted the teachers who worked with their children to use sign language with the children.*

*Ms. Galway began investigating this strategy because she was hopeful that children would be less frustrated when trying to communicate their needs if they could use simple hand signs for food, drink, and so forth.*

*The parents overwhelmingly responded that they were in favor of the teachers using sign language with their children. As a result of this survey, the teachers began using simple signs with all children in the infant and toddler rooms while collecting information on the frustration levels of the children.*

*In this case, the issue was the inability of the children to communicate their feelings. Based on the data collected through the parent survey, the use of sign language in the infant and toddler room continued. This resulted in a drastic reduction in student frustration.*

Although the vast majority of action research involves teacher-facilitated inquiry, at times questions will lead you to seek information from parents. The results of the project led to a change in how the classroom teachers worked with infants and toddlers on a daily basis, and the parents were encouraged to follow the same practices with their child at home. As a follow-up to this project, some parents asked for more information on using sign language with young children, and this could lead to additional questions about the actual use of sign language at home and its impact on classroom use of sign language.

### Case 4: Ms. Roper's Reader's Theater

*Ms. Roper, a preservice teacher of second and third grade students, designed an action research project to address the reading deficits of a group of students.*

*Six eight-year-old, third grade students who struggled with both reading fluency and comprehension worked in a small group using a Reader's Theater approach in her required action research project. A decoding skill was taught, practiced, and then applied through the use of repeated readings of Reader's Theater Scripts with these six students. Additionally, comprehension was assessed weekly by having students answer four multiple choice questions and one short answer question related to the Reader's Theater Script.*

*The assessment results showed an increase in oral fluency and retelling proficiency in five of the six students and an increased confidence in their reading ability. The outcome of this case was the anticipated result, but it also led to several other questions for further research, which included: Was the increased fluency a result of the repeated readings or the small group instruction? Was the increased fluency the result of the motivation level of the students? Was the increased comprehension the result of the design layout of a script? These questions illustrate the cyclical nature of action research and show how assessing the outcome of implementing one action can lead to future topics for research and action.*

The identified issue in this project was that the students were not fluent readers and, due to their lack of fluency, their comprehension was compromised. The correlation between fluency and comprehension was established through research and then appropriate actions were planned to address the deficits. Skill specific scripts were obtained to use for the needed decoding skills and the skill was taught to the group. Each student was assigned a character for the script and then, through repeated readings, the students were able to practice the skill.

Anecdotal records showed that the students struggled with the application of the newly learned decoding skill in the initial reading but began applying it more consistently with each additional reading. The records also showed that the students continued to apply the skill in consecutive weeks after new skills were taught.

## Case 5: Ms. Hogan's Math Class

*A teacher of first and second graders was looking for an alternative strategy to use for increasing her students mastery of the basic math facts.*

*Ms. Hogan decided to teach her thirty students how to use a calculator and then give them various basic addition equations to solve using a calculator, on a daily basis, for twenty days. Students were required to enter the equation in the calculator and record the answer in the hopes that the repeated practice would help the students memorize the facts.*

*Pre- and post-assessments were used to identify if the actions taken were effective in meeting the issue addressed by the project. The data was collected and analyzed and in this case, there was no consistent evidence that the action taken increased the students' achievement.*

Ms. Hogan's actions didn't produce the desired outcome of increasing student mastery. However, her findings were valuable in providing information for what her next action could be. It was apparent that the repeated practice and exposure was not an effective method for increasing mastery on a consistent basis, so it was back to the drawing board.

Ms. Hogan knew that the issue of students needing to master these basic facts were/are crucial foundations for more complex learning. She continued her action research. Ms. Hogan found that by singing the basic facts, or and applying some movement to each fact (strategies she found in professional literature), improved students memorization skills.

## Case Studies' Summary

These five case studies demonstrate that although the issues impacting infants to eight year olds may have varying nuances, the course of action a reflective practitioner follows when addressing the issue at hand is the same. From frustration at not being able to communicate well, to mastery of the basic addition facts, the issues were identified first, and then the stages for action research (described in chapter 1) were followed. You will find that even though certain age learners portray unique characters in the action research story being told, the desired outcome of identifying and using the right strategies at the right time, and creating positive and effective learning experience students, are universal goals in the educational environment.

## APPLYING THE ACTION RESEARCH PROCESS
## IN YOUR EARLY CHILDHOOD CLASSROOM SETTING

### Step 1. Issue Identification

In chapter 1, you read about ways to identify issues you might pursue as action research questions. Although similar to questions posed at the elementary and secondary levels, your questions may be slightly different because of the age and skill levels of the children with which you are working. You will find that any formal or informal setting can provide initial opportunities for both research and action. For example, as you conduct circle time activities in a nursery school setting or during direct instruction in the first grade classroom, the children may not participate in the manner that you had intended. You can initiate an action research study by simply asking yourself questions such as:

- When did things begin to go a direction that was not part of my plan?
- How did I react to children's behaviors during this time?
- Who were the children who were not actively participating in the activities?
- What could I do differently the next time I call children together?
- Did the location create problems?
- What were my expectations for children's learning? Did I meet my expectations?
- Were there distractions that kept the children from fully participating in the activities? What were those distractions and how can I minimize them?
- What can I do to help the child(ren) with special needs become more active participants?

As you begin to focus on a particular aspect of your classroom, you will likely find that you raise questions about other areas. A focus on one area such as whole group time might lead you to uncovering more specific issues. For example, as you ask the question, "I wonder what would happen if I can reduce problematic behaviors?" You may discover that making a change in group time will impact the rest of your daily schedule. The change in schedule may, in turn, lead you to discover that the longer time spent in learning centers results in inappropriate behaviors because children don't have enough to keep them busy at the centers.

Another way of forming your questions may come from looking at the children in their learning environment through questions like, "How would adding a discovery center affect children's ability to ask 'scientific' questions?" For more ideas or reflection on teacher research conducted in early childhood settings, you can also visit "Voices of Practitioners" found on the National Association for the Education of Young Children (NAEYC) Web site. You will find action research conducted by teachers on a variety of topics that may inspire your thinking.

## Step 2. Data Collection: Documentation Forms

Collecting samples of what children have done can provide useful information to explore your questions. For years teachers collected samples of children's work from the beginning of the year until the end of the year and now we speak about keeping portfolios of the children's work. Comparing a self-portrait from the first week of attendance with a self-portrait a year later can demonstrate a child's fine motor growth and understanding of self.

Comparing samples of children's stories, perhaps first dictated to teachers and later self-written, can show children's understanding of story concepts. Even keeping samples of children's attempts at writing can be useful to document how the children are progressing. Having this type of documentation is invaluable when you are reporting your findings and drawing your conclusions about your research focus.

Photographs can be a great format for recording the events in your classroom and can be used in a number of ways. One use might be to document children's work in the block area so that they can rebuild and refine their structure on future days. Photographs of block creations may help you document children's developing understanding of physics or mathematics.

When photographs can be accompanied by children's language, you will have even more data to provide you insight into children's thinking. This is where video or audio recording may prove quite useful. It is one thing to have a still photo or written description of what you are seeing, but it adds a new dimension when you have children's actual words to add to your data. Videotape often permits the researcher to not only see what children are doing, but also to have the advantage of capturing the children's "language" as they interact with materials; this can be critical to accurate and affective assessment (Huber 1997).

The use of checklists, another excellent source of data, allows you to quickly determine if a child possesses specific behaviors, skills, or characteristics. As you complete checklists, you may discover that you are focusing on certain skills more than others. This data might cue you to adjust your plans to address neglected skills. Typically, however, checklists will only provide information on whether or not the behavior, skill, or characteristic is observed. They do not tell you how well the child demonstrates that skill, behavior, or characteristic. Checklists may help you discover trends about the children in your classroom. This might lead to a research question and further action research.

### Step 3. Action Planning: Special Considerations in Early Childhood Action Research

As you have read and are aware of by now, action research is a process that follows a pretty well organized set of steps, however, there are a few special considerations for working with young children.

*Consideration 1: Cognition*

Early childhood educators are well aware that working with young children and their families may be different in many ways from working with older children. Early childhood learners are unique individuals with a very different ways of looking at, and making sense of, the environment around them. Central to any conversation or interaction must be the understanding that these children are concrete thinkers who often don't realize things exist if they can't touch them. Things that may not impact older individuals can have a huge impact on young children for their higher order thinking strategies are not yet fully developed.

When doing action research with early childhood learners, you must take into consideration the developmental level of the child. Just because some children are able to master a skill does not mean that it is developmentally appropriate for that aged child, so it is important that any generalization regarding skills are based in the normal behavior trends and not the exceptional behaviors that you may observe.

*Consideration 2: Documentation*

Documenting your work with nonverbal or children with limited expressive and receptive language skills is challenging. You cannot conduct an interview with an infant, but you may find other ways to document responses from infants.

The increased affordability and availability of digital and video make it very easy to document the responses of young children. Children may not be able to write words or sentences but pictures often tell a detailed story of their thinking. Anecdotal records, such as you might keep in a teacher-as-research journal are a valuable source of documentation. As already discussed, checklists can also provide you with excellent information about your young children. Documentation systems may even vary from child to child based on their developmental level, but the common thread is that you are consistently documenting your actions, as well as the impact of these action, on children.

### Consideration 3: The Relationship between the Child and Teacher

Because teachers as action researchers are directly involved with their students during action research, the relationship between the teacher and child has an undeniable impact on growth and development. To get the most accurate information for reflection and action planning, it is beneficial to establish a trusting relationship with the child.

Very often, young children answer questions from adults with how they perceive the adult would want them to answer. Since it is possible to manipulate children to answer as you would like, you may want to have the children share in decisions related to their involvement in or in the process of the research. This may be as simple as asking the children for their permission to participate in your data collection. You may want to tell children that you will be trying out something new to see what will happen. While this may seem like a trite detail, if you are planning to interview children you will want them to be willing participants.

### Consideration 4: Context

Another consideration in planning your action research is context. Children bring to your classroom a variety of experiences and those experiences impact their ability to understand some concepts. A child who has traveled extensively will have a different understanding of the world than a child who has lived in an urban area and never traveled outside of their neighborhood. A child who has been read to regularly will bring a general knowledge of books for greater than a child who enters school having never seen a book.

It is important to remember that "context" goes far beyond experiences and includes such things as culture, socioeconomic conditions, and learning abilities, to name of a few. Thus, it is important to consider the context of your classroom when identifying issues and planning you actions. When you have questions, remember that there is a wealth of information available on the NAEYC (National Association for the Education of Young Learners) Web site.

### Consideration 5: Parent Involvement

If you choose to involve parents in your action research, you will need to consider how you will motivate parents to complete a questionnaire or interview. While some parents may readily provide you with information, other parents may be less willing to respond to your request. Some parents may have difficulty reading a questionnaire due to language barriers or reading difficulty so you may find it helpful to have a translator assist in the development of the questionnaire or have the parent respond orally to the questionnaire.

You may also want to provide a special place to conduct an interview privately and/or provide an incentive to encourage parent participation. As you become familiar with the parents of the children in your classroom, you will be able to determine what incentives, if any, might be appropriate. One other word of caution is that parents often aren't familiar with some of the "buzz words" of the educators so it is always helpful to have a non-educator review your questions.

### Consideration 6: The Child/Children

Often, the best way to find out answers to your questions is to go right to the source and ask the child(ren) directly. However with young children, this method poses a variety of challenges. Depending on your question, you may have specific predetermined questions that you ask each child or you may use a set of questions and adjust the questions you ask based on children's responses.

Should you decide to interview preschool children, you will want to be aware of potential pitfalls with this format. You may encounter children who want to please you and thus will want to give you the "right" answer even if a right answer does not exist. The other end of the spectrum would be the child who is only concerned about completing the interview and will give any answer in an effort to get on with another activity. Children's vocabulary and/or language skills may be limited and thus influence your data collection. Keep in mind that young children can be easily distracted and you may have difficulty keeping them on topic during an interview or discussion. Each format for gathering information has some issues and you will want to take those into consideration as you plan your action research study.

Anecdotal records can help you become aware of children's behavior, interests, or development over time. Crucial to anecdotal records is that you have a specific focus and that you compile observations at regular intervals. If you leave the focus too general, you may not notice changes in the child.

For example, if you intend to focus on development, but are not specific, you may not be aware that a child has accomplished a development goal such as tying his shoes or managing his own clothing during potty training. If you are examining child characteristics such as motivation, your anecdotal records need to reflect factors that appear to impact the motivation of the child(ren) such as minor health factors like allergies, colds, teething, and so on. Always remember that just as adults are impacted by a lack of sleep or allergies, the little ones are probably more impacted by those minor occurrences.

Determining the best method for finding the answer to your research questions is an important consideration as well. Many of your answers will be found by observing children, but it is important to keep in mind that children's actions are framed within the culture of your particular classroom and their family life.

When you consider the actions by children in your classroom, you will want to consider the interactions of children that might lead a child to act a particular way. Each child brings aspects of his or her community and family to any classroom interaction. Two children presented with the same situation may respond very differently based on values or intention along with many other influences. For example, one child may respond to anther's verbal insult by hitting the offending child, while another may respond with, "I don't like it when you say that." One way of looking at this would be to say that the first child is aggressive and the second is more intellectual in response; however, another way of looking at this might be to consider how you (or others) respond to children when they insult other children.

Young children do not inherently know how to respond to unpleasant situations and have to be taught appropriate reactions. If a child has witnessed hitting as a response to verbal confrontations, that child has learned that hitting is an accepted response. Yet when children are given the words to say in response to another child hitting them or saying something to them, they have the skills to respond verbally to the insult and will be less likely to hit. It is through repeated exposures and education that young children learn how to respond to situations, and it is important to be factual and nonjudgmental in reporting observations.

*Consideration 7: YOU!*

While you personally develop as an educator, your perceptions and attitudes have been influenced by the textbooks you have read and the instructors who have taught you. You will also need to consider those influences and the impact they will have on any research you conduct.

If Jean Piaget's work is the basis for your beliefs, you are likely to frame your questions from the viewpoint that children are capable and competent learners whose development follows stages. If you are more familiar with the work of Maria Montessori, you may approach your questions with considerations about how to prepare the environment or children's decision-making. Those who have read the work of Lev Vygotsky may focus on children's interactions and the social component to learning or how to keep children in what he termed the "Zone of Proximal Development" (Bodrova

& Leong, 2007). Those who have influenced education are too numerous to list, but be cognizant that your perceptions are framed on what you have learned and believe.

## Step 4. Plan Activation: Finding Out What You Want to Know!

Now is the moment of truth, for the time to implement your action is now! You have researched your issue, identified interventions, planned for potential problems, gathered the needed materials, and developed record keeping strategies. Now is the time to use all the knowledge you have gained to start acting on your research. Put your plan in motion and keep in mind the cyclical nature of action research. Just remember, that very often one action will lead to another and the cycle of action research will continue.

Do not be discouraged if your anticipated outcome doesn't materialize: instead just modify your actions and keep moving. You will find your answers and both you and your students will benefit from your reflections and actions! Congratulations—You are now in the process of completing the nitty-gritty of an "action research" project!

## Step 5. Outcome Assessment

At this point you may have answered your original question or may have even more questions. This is to be expected and is part of the cyclical nature of action research described in chapter 1.

You have identified an issue, collected your data, planned and implemented your action, collected more data, and now you can either share what you have learned or begin the process again based on the new questions you have. Either way, you have completed the process with even the youngest members of society and lived to talk about it.

The children from birth to age eight may be young and innocent, but the opportunities and possibilities for conducting action research are almost endless. With every new beginning or class, you gain a new opportunity to build a solid and secure foundation for all future learning with the children you work with through action research.

## PERSONAL LEARNING

If you are interested in your own growth or learning as a teacher, you might find keeping a personal journal effective for collecting information and detailing your journey. You may find it helpful to record what you are thinking, feeling, experiencing. You may use a journal to record your observations or the interactions of the children in your classroom. Reflecting on these at a future time may provide valuable insight into your area of focus or concern. As a reflective practioner, a journal is an effective means for documenting and reviewing what you are doing.

## CONCLUSION

Action research is a valuable tool in the early childhood classroom. When you incorporate this practice into you repertoire of skills, you will find that you can learn a great deal about your classroom, your students, and even yourself!

You may need to give some extra thought and attention to framing your questions and collecting your data, but you can identify issues and find answers to questions in any early childhood setting just as you can with other age learners. As stated earlier, the first eight years of a child's life are when the foundation for all future learning is built. Use your role as an educator and reflective practioner to ensure that the foundation being built is solid, is constructed of the best practices, and is developmentally appropriate for the youngest learners. You are the voice for young children. Conducting action research may not only answer your questions, but may also lead you to advocate for appropriate policies and practices for young children.

## QUESTIONS FOR REVIEW AND REFLECTION

1. Describe the evolution of action research in early childhood settings.
2. How can your teaching reflections lead to you to potential action research questions?
3. What are the special considerations when conducting action research in an early childhood setting? How does one address these challenges?
4. In what ways might questions around school readiness guide your development of an action research study in your early childhood setting?

## REFERENCES

Bodrova, E. & Leong, D. (2007). *Tools of the mind: The Vygotskian approach to early childhood education* (2nd ed.). Columbus, OH: Pearson Merrill Prentice-Hall.

Grace, D. & Brandt, M. (2006). Ready for success in kindergarten: A comparative analysis of teacher, parent, and administrator beliefs in Hawaii. *Journal of Early Childhood Research, 4*(3), 223–58.

Graue, M. E. & Walsh, D. J. (1995). Children in context: Interpreting the here and now of children's lives. In Hatch, J. A. (Ed.), *Qualitative research in early childhood settings.* (pp. 135–54) Westport, CT: Praeger Publishers.

Harris, K. & Knudsen-Lindauer, S. (1988). Parental and teacher priorities for kindergarten preparation. *Child Study Journal, 18*(2), 61–73.

Hatch, J. A. (Ed.) (1995). *Qualitative research in early childhood settings.* Westport, CT: Praeger Publishers.

Hatch, J. A., Greer, T., & Bailey, K. (2006). Student produced action research in early childhood teacher education. *Journal of Early Childhood Teacher Education, 27*(2), 205–12.

Huber (Taylor), L. (1997). Children's language and sociodramatic play with multicultural materials. Unpublished doctoral dissertation. Ball State University.

Lara-Cinisomo, S., Fuligni, A. S., Ritchie, S., Howes, C., & Karoly, L. (2008). Getting ready for school: An examination of early childhood educators' belief systems. *Early Childhood Education Journal, 35*(4), 343–49.

Katz, L. & Chard, S. (2000). *Engaging in children's minds: The project approach* (2nd ed.). Stamford, CT: Ablex Publishing.

Lasky, L. (1978). Personalized teaching: Action research in action. *Young Children, 33*(3), 58–64.

Malaguzzi, L. (1998). History, ideas, and basic philosophy: An interview with Lella Gandini. In Edwards, C., Gandini, L., & Forman, G. (Eds.) (1998). *The hundred languages of children: The Reggio Emilia approach—Advanced reflections* (2nd ed.) Westport, CT: Ablex Publishing.

Maxwell, K., & Clifford, R. (2004). School readiness assessment. *Young Children, 59*(1), 42–46.

Meier, D. & Henderson, B. (2007). Learning from young children in the classroom: The art and science of teacher research. New York, NY: Teachers College Press.

Paley, V. G. (1981). *Wally's stories.* Cambridge, MA: Harvard University Press.

Piotrkowski, C., Botsko, M., & Matthews, E. (2000). Parents and teachers beliefs about children's school readiness in a high-need community. *Early Childhood Research Quarterly, 15*(4), 537–58.

Rust, F. O'Connell. (2007). Action research in early childhood contexts. In Hatch, J. (Ed.), *Early childhood qualitative research.* New York: Routledge.

Saluja G., Scott-Little, C., & Clifford, R. (2000). Readiness for school: A survey of state policies and definitions. *Early Childhood Research & Practice, 2*(2). Retrieved from http://ecrp.uiuc.edu/v2n2/saluja.html.

# 5

# Action Research through the Lens of Lesson Study

*Catherine C. Lewis, PhD, Distinguished Research Scholar and Director, Lesson Study Group, Mills College, Oakland, California*

*Elizabeth K. Baker, PhD, Visiting Assistant Professor Mathematics and Science Education, Department of Education, Mills College, Oakland, California*

> Improving something as complex and culturally embedded as teaching requires the efforts of all the players, including students, parents, and politicians. But teachers must be the primary driving force behind change. They are the best positioned to understand the problems that students face and to generate possible solutions.
>
> —Stigler & Hiebert (1999, p. 135)

## INTRODUCTION

This chapter provides an introduction to lesson study, an action research approach that has spread rapidly in North America since its introduction from Japan in 1999. Lesson study, like other forms of action research, follows a series of stages or "phases" and is cyclical in nature. In a lesson study cycle, teachers work together to consider their long-term goals for students, bring those goals to life in actual "research lessons," and carefully observe and discuss student learning during the lessons, drawing out implications for the teaching of a topic and for teaching and learning more broadly.

In Japan, lesson study is routinely practiced by both preservice and in-service educators in all subject areas, and has been credited for the evolution of effective and widely shared mathematics and science teaching techniques (C. Lewis 2000; C. Lewis & Tsuchida 1997; Shimizu 2002; Takahashi 2000).

Although lesson study first received widespread attention in the United States in conjunction with the Third International Mathematics and Science Study (Stigler & Hiebert 1999), practitioner-led lesson study groups have emerged in a wide variety of subject areas including language arts, environmental studies, history, and music (Hurd & Licciardo-Musso 2005; Ogden, Perkins, & Donahue 2008; Pesick 2005). A number of U.S. teacher education programs include lesson study within coursework on curriculum and instruction, content, or teaching methods (Baker 2007; Cossey & Tucher 2005; Finken, Matthews, Hlas, & Schmidt 2004; Hiebert, Morris, & Glass 2003; J. Lewis 2007; Perry, Tucher, & Lewis 2003; Taylor & Puchner 2003)

## CHAPTER OBJECTIVES

By the time you finish reading and thinking about this chapter you will be able to:

- Describe each phase of the lesson study cycle
- Explain what the *lesson* in lesson study means
- Utilize activities that will help you anticipate student thinking
- Use the lesson study tools included in this chapter to set norms, develop a research theme, develop a teaching-learning plan for the research lesson, and observe and conduct a research lesson

## OVERVIEW OF LESSON STUDY

### The Lesson Study Process

The lesson study is a simple idea. If you want to improve instruction, what could be more obvious than collaborating with fellow teachers to plan and examine lessons? While it may be a simple idea, lesson study is a challenging process, since it asks teachers to reveal their content knowledge and beliefs about good teaching, to collaboratively develop a lesson plan, and to focus on *student thinking and learning* during observation of live instruction.

In lesson study, a team of four to six teachers works together to:

- Consider their long-term goals for student learning and development, and identify gaps between these long-term goals and current reality. Based on this gap, team members develop a research theme for their lesson study work.

- Identify a topic of interest in student learning, and study the curriculum and underlying content knowledge related to that topic, as well as related research, data on student learning, and other relevant materials (such as standards).
- Within the topic of interest, choose a unit and lesson to focus on and collaboratively plan out one research lesson within the unit, using it to bring to life what is known about this subject matter and its teaching-learning.
- Conduct the research lesson, with one team member teaching and others gathering data on student learning and development.
- In a post-lesson discussion, share and discuss the data gathered during the lesson, drawing out implications for lesson and unit design and for teaching and learning more broadly.
- (If desired, revise the lesson, teach it in another classroom, and study and improve it again.) [1]

Figure 5.1 provides an overview of the teacher-led instructional improvement cycle that constitutes lesson study.

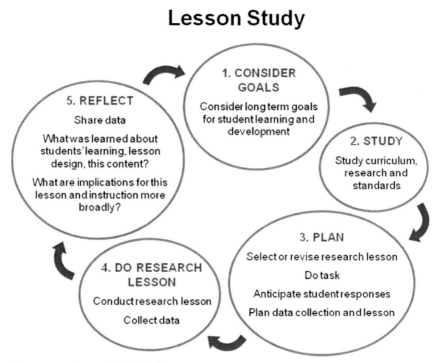

## Lesson Study

**Figure 5.1.   Lesson Study Cycle**

| Phases of Lesson Study | Steps in Action Research |
| --- | --- |
| Consider Goals | Issue Identification |
| Study | Data Collection |
| Plan | Action Planning |
| Do Research Lesson | Plan Activation |
| Reflect | Outcome Assessment |

**Figure 5.2. Lesson Study Action Research**

At this point, you probably are already beginning to see how the innate fundamentals of action research are embedded within the lesson study design as shown in figure 5.2.

## LESSON STUDY TOOLS

Lesson study often asks teachers to move outside their comfort zone, so tools to support new ways of working together are essential. Tools included in this chapter include protocols for norm setting, development of a shared research theme, data collection on student learning and behavior, and discussion of the research lesson.

The tools of lesson study are designed to support teachers in training who want to "learn and do" action research, as Pelton describes in the preface of this book, and for the college instructors, supervisors, and administrators who seek to support teachers in training. Further detail of these tools are available in handbooks devoted to a much more comprehensive view of lesson study (C. Lewis 2002; Wang-Iverson & Yoshida 2005) at several Web sites (see www.lessonresearch.net for links) and also in videos that show lesson study cycles conducted by both U.S. and Japanese teachers (Mills College Lesson Study Group 2000, 2005). Appendix A provides a sample schedule for integration of lesson study into a preservice course.

## LAYING THE GROUNDWORK FOR YOUR LESSON STUDY

Even before embarking on what this volume regards as the first phase of action research—issue identification—we suggest that you develop ground rules for your work together, as described in this section. Some activities within lesson study—such as joint examination of content knowledge, collaborative lesson planning and observation, and discussion of lessons—may actually be more familiar to teacher candidates than to in-service U.S. teachers. However, the types of lesson planning and observation that occur

What will make this lesson study group a supportive and productive site for your learning?

- Jot down a list of characteristics important to you. (It may help to think about characteristics of groups that have functioned well—or poorly—to support your learning in the past.) You may want to consider some general norms (such as listening and taking responsibility) and some that have been identified as especially important to your content area. For example, in mathematics, norms like the following may assume importance:
  - Exploring and "unpacking" mathematical connections, being curious;
  - Explaining and justifying solutions, agreeing on what constitutes an adequate justification
  - Evaluating solution strategies for correctness, efficiency, and insight
  - Expressing agreement or disagreement (Ball & Bass, 2000a, 2000b; Ball, Bass, Hill, & Thames, 2006; Cobb, Yackel, & Wood, 1989; Cobb, Stephan, McClain, & Gravemeijer, 2001).

- Share and discuss ideas as a group, acknowledging the ideas generated by each member, taking particular care to identify and discuss any possible contradictions. For example, if one group member asks for a "safe environment to share my ideas" and another for " a group that will continuously challenge my thinking," talk about how both desires can be honored.
- Synthesize members' ideas to a group list of about 5 key norms you all support.
- Record the norms for future reference.

**Figure 5.3.  Developing Norms for Your Lesson Study Work**

during lesson study are often quite different from those that occur in other preservice activities, so it is important to develop norms (agreed-upon ground rules) that will support the work. Figure 5.3 suggests a process for developing norms with your group, modeled on effective groups observed in the San Mateo–Foster City School District in California.

The following examples of norms from teacher candidates and in-service teachers in Berkeley, and Oakland, California, may provide a useful starting point to think about the kinds of norms that will be useful for your group:

- Show respect for each other's ideas and also be willing to challenge and be challenged.
- Keep comments focused on the student learning.
- When talking about students, speak about them as if they or their parents are in the room.
- Open your mind to other viewpoints.
- Stay on task.

- No side conversations.
- Rotate administrative responsibilities.
- Come prepared to work hard.

We recommend that your group develop norms and at the beginning of each meeting choose one or more norm to self-monitor during the meeting. (Each group member may want to silently identify a norm, or you can do this as a group if you wish.) At the end of the meeting, discuss whether the norm was upheld and what can be improved in the group process so that the norm can be upheld in the future. The segment "Sticking to the Process" on the video *How Many Seats?* shows how one group of U.S. teachers honed their group's working processes by monitoring and reflecting on norms (C. Lewis, Perry, & Hurd 2009; Mills College Lesson Study Group 2005).

In addition to setting norms, teachers in the San Mateo–Foster City School District recommend choosing roles—for example, facilitator, chart recorder, electronic note taker—and rotating them at each meeting. They also suggest that each lesson study meeting begin with a review of the prior meeting's minutes, and that each meeting end by summarizing the learning from the meeting, outlining the work that needs to be accomplished at the next meeting, and reflecting on the monitored norm.

## GETTING STARTED WITH YOUR LESSON STUDY

### Phase 1 of Lesson Study: Consider Your Long-Term Goals for Student Learning and Development

The first task of lesson study is to develop a *research theme* to guide the lesson study work. The research theme allows teachers to voice their long-term aspirations for students and come to a shared set of goals. Figure 5.4 provides a step-by-step guide to developing a research theme.

Each part of the task should be presented separately, before looking at the next part. Typically, the research theme is developed by all the teachers at a school or all the members of a preservice class, based on careful observation of the strengths and challenges of students they teach. Development of the research theme is to help us reconnect with our long-term goals for student development and to identify gaps between these goals and students' current characteristics.

While at first blush, the process of developing a research theme may not seem relevant to learning of specific academic subject matter, it lays the groundwork for lesson study and for focus on academic learning in three important ways. First, participants can focus on qualities crucial to students' *long-term* development as learners that may be neglected in daily planning,

**Part 1:**
**Think about the students you serve. What qualities would you like those students to have 5-10 years from now? Jot down a list of the qualities you would like your students to have if you were to meet them 5-10 years from now.**
*Present this prompt separately, verbally or visually, before looking at the prompts below. Have participants discuss their lists.*

**Part 2:**
**Once again, call to mind the students you serve. List their current qualities. Think about their strengths as well as any qualities you may find worrisome. Make a second list of your students' current qualities.**
*Present this prompt separately, verbally or visually, before looking at the prompts below. Have participants discuss their lists.*

**Part 3:**
**Compare the ideal and the actual qualities you listed. Identify a gap between the ideal and the actual that you strongly feel merits your attention as an educator.**
*Have participants briefly work individually, and then share their ideas with the group.*

**Part 4:**
**Collaboratively develop a research theme—that is, a long-term goal—for your lesson study work, by stating positively the ideal student qualities you wish to build. For example, teachers at a school serving low-achieving students whose families had suffered discrimination chose the following goal:**
*"Our students will develop fundamental academic skills that will ensure their progress and a strong sense of human rights."*

**Figure 5.4.   Developing the Research Theme for Lesson Study**

such as curiosity, persistence, or the habit of thinking mathematically (or historically, scientifically, etc.) in daily life.

By developing a research theme, teacher candidates have the opportunity to think about how their daily instructional practice relates to their long-term goals and to shape a data collection plan of student qualities that will support long-term academic learning and development as well as immediate learning. As one teacher candidate at Mills College noted:

> A lot of [American] schools develop mission statements, but we don't do anything with them. The mission statements get put in a drawer and then teachers become cynical because the mission statements don't go anywhere. Lesson study gives guts to a mission statement, makes it real, and brings it to life. [2]

Second, the process of developing the research theme allows teacher candidates to carefully consider their students: Who are they, and what are their strengths and challenges? As teacher candidates share ideas, they can compare their own views of students with those held by colleagues. For example, teacher candidates described their sixth, seventh, and eighth grade students as curious and eager to learn new ways of thinking about science, but described tenth grade students as typically disaffected.

Third, development of the research theme provides motivational fuel, by connecting teacher candidates' most central goals—such as building motivation to learn—to the particular topic under study. The long-term focus of the research theme provides a welcome counterbalance to the short-term focus of much educational evaluation, reminding us that it is important to know not just whether students have learned to perform a particular procedure, but whether they have learned to do it in a way likely to foster continued development of mathematical (or historical, analytic, scientific, etc.) habits of mind.

For prospective teacher candidates, the research theme also provides a way of coming to know learners through the eyes of colleagues who work with students from other sites, grade levels, and socioeconomic contexts. Each teacher candidate brings knowledge about a different school environment and different learners, and the process of developing the research theme gives teacher candidates an opportunity to articulate, negotiate, and refine beliefs about student learning before entering the challenging realm of planning the research lesson.

### Example from Mills College

Lesson study has been an integral part of the year-long Mills College post-graduate mathematics and science secondary credential program since 2001 (Baker 2007; Cossey & Tucher 2005; Perry et al. 2003). Teacher candidates work in placements that range from middle school to high school and across a broad socioeconomic range, so it is often challenging for them to arrive at a shared research theme. During the first class of the semester each prospective teacher identifies one (*just* one) personal teaching goal, writes about that goal, and then shares the goal with classmates. A sample of goals from one class illustrates the wide range of personal goals, from classroom management and behavioral issues, to content:

- I want my students to persist through the nitty gritty of setting up their data recording. They easily get defeated and say, "this experiment is not working," and begin guessing how the lab should turn out.
- I want to get better at classroom management; some of my students are on task but many are just coasting in class or are disrupting the learning of others.
- I want to understand student engagement because my students seem so uninterested in mathematics; they just want to know enough to pass the tests.

- My goal is to teach my students that there are benefits to struggling with an idea. They seem to want instant understanding and just be done with it.
- I would like to my students to ask more questions about the concepts, not just accept what I say, so my goal is to get better at presenting material in a way that gets my students asking questions. When I teach the content, they need to make sense of it for their own lives.
- I'm not sure if my students really understand the mathematics or if they just are good at memorizing formulas and taking the tests, so I would say my goal is to really understand what exactly they are learning, because in the long run, it won't be good enough to just know the formula.

Voicing their personal teaching goals out loud to their peers helps teacher candidates identify what ideas they have in common and reveals how individual concerns connect to group ideas about student learning. After this discussion of their own pressing questions and key challenges, teacher candidates can quickly proceed with the steps outlined in figure 5.4. The teacher candidates in this example arrived at a shared research theme that read:

> Students will actively participate, express curiosity, and demonstrate responsibility for their own learning so that they can communicate their understanding through a team effort.

While this goal might seem like a mouthful, its development provided an important opportunity for participants to see teaching through each other's eyes and to consider the many goals of education. The teacher candidates hypothesized that the research lesson could support the research theme by creating a context in which student participation and ideas are valued, even in the case of mistakes or shortcomings. The teacher candidates agreed that the tasks and activities they chose for the lesson must allow for each student to demonstrate and communicate their understanding to their peers and also to the teacher.

By thinking about their own personal goals and their colleagues' goals for their students at the outset, the teacher candidates focused not simply on the lesson activity but also on how the lesson would build students' long-term development. As one teacher candidate commented:

> This [process] has opened up different approaches and new ways of identifying valuable learning trajectories for me and for my students, and I think that's really exciting. This kind of analysis can keep me fresh and current and not stale.[3]

## Phase 2 of Lesson Study:
## Selection of Topic and Study of Content

Phase 2 is selection and study of the topic that will be the focus of the research lesson. This phase provides a chance to study in depth some element of the curriculum. A topic may be well suited to lesson study for many different reasons, such as because it is:

- persistently difficult for students or for teacher candidates to understand deeply,
- challenging to teach,
- central to the curriculum, or
- just happens to be taught at a convenient time for the research lesson.

Diagnostic tests and other types of student assessments may clearly identify a problem in student learning that would provide a good focus for lesson study. For you to settle on a topic, it may be useful to look at data from your teaching placements, such as assessments or classroom work, or to administer a task to students and bring back the data to your lesson study group. Your supervising teachers and mentor teachers may be good resources to help identify a topic to work on.

Often, further study of the problem and of existing curricula and research (as described later in this section) will shift or build your group's understanding about what exactly is the problem in student leaning. For example, one group of lower elementary teachers originally thought their students were having difficulty with the place value of ones and tens, but as they began to design a lesson, they found that the real problem seemed to be students' fluency with number combinations up to twenty.

The point of the lesson study cycle is not simply to produce a lesson, but to study the topic and student thinking related to that topic in considerable depth. To deepen knowledge of the topic you have chosen to study, it will be useful for your lesson study group to:

- Carefully review your own curriculum materials and national and state standards, especially any supporting materials in the teacher's manual designed to build in-depth content knowledge.
- Compare your curriculum with a different curriculum (perhaps one that is strongly research based or is recommended by a national subject matter organization), in order to find contrasting approaches and to further illuminate how students might learn this particular content.
- Read relevant research.

The following guiding questions will be useful:

- What are the important understandings that our students need to develop about this topic and how do they develop?
- What do students currently understand about this topic, and what experiences will help build bridges from current understanding to new understanding?
- How do different curricula treat this topic, and what are the advantages and disadvantages of each?

Teacher education faculty often design their classes to help teacher candidates learn about student misconceptions and about recent innovations in teaching practice. Lesson study is an excellent opportunity to revisit and dig deeper into articles and texts assigned to you, follow up on the footnotes in articles of interest to your group, spend time at the Web sites of subject matter associations, and put your questions to your faculty and supervising teachers.

Lesson study groups of practicing teachers often include an outside specialist, such as a teacher or researcher who is knowledgeable about the subject matter under study and how to teach it. In lesson study, the role of the outside specialist is to raise questions, add new perspectives, and act as a co-researcher, but not to direct the group. If you are participating in a lesson study group as a teacher candidate, your education faculty is aware of this distinction, but others may not be.

**Phase 3: Develop the Teaching-Learning Plan**

Do not think you must write a lesson from scratch. Lesson study is most productive when educators use and refine good existing lessons, rather than reinventing the wheel. Figure 5.5 provides a template for the teaching-learning plan for the research lesson. Spend some time looking it over and discuss this question:

What are the similarities and differences between the teaching-learning plan template in figure 5.5 and lesson plans familiar to you?

If at all possible, look at a completed version of a teaching-learning plan at a lesson study Web site (such as www.lessonresearch.net; lessonstudy-group.net; or globaledresources.com).

To maximize the feeling of working together on "our lesson," many U.S. lesson study groups defer the decision of who will teach the research lesson until just before the research lesson is taught. Teacher candidates at Mills College found this to be disconcerting at first; as one teacher put it, "These

Use the following as prompts and record your information on separate paper.

Team Members:
Instructor:
Date:
Grade Level:

1. Title of Lesson:

2. Goals (3 Levels: Research Theme, Broad Subject-Matter Goals, Lesson Goals)

3. Lesson Rationale: Why we chose to focus on this topic and goals. (For example, what is difficult about learning/teaching this topic? What do we notice about students currently as learners?) Why we designed the lesson as shown below.

4. How does students' understanding of this topic develop? For example, how does this lesson fit within a unit? How does it fit within students' experiences in prior and subsequent grades?

5. Relationship of the lesson to State Standards

6. Lesson Design:

| Student Learning Activities | Anticipated Student Reponses and Teacher Support | Points to Notice (Evaluation) |
|---|---|---|
|  |  |  |

7. Data collection points during the lesson observation.
   • Our team will collect data on:

   • Outside observers are asked to collect data on:

**Figure 5.5.   Teaching-Learning Plan for the Research Lesson**

are my kids, this is my school! I know best what will work for them." However, at the conclusion of the topic study she reflected:

> I am so relieved to have been able to focus on content. It was a luxury not to worry about the daily logistics, routines, and plans to teach. Now, I'm sure anyone of us could teach my class. I see my kids' strengths and weaknesses in a new light.[4]

The teaching-learning plan has several functions. It:

- provides a guide for the teacher of the research lesson,
- captures and shares your group's learning and thinking about the topic,
- provides a guide for observers, letting them know how to focus their data collection during the lesson, and
- provides a roadmap of your lesson study action research, by explaining why you chose to focus on this topic, why you designed the lesson as you did, and how your design relates to your long-term goals for students.

Typically, three different levels of goals are found in a teaching-learning plan. Examples taken from teacher candidate lesson-study groups follow.

### Research Theme or Main Aim

- Take initiative to learn and to support the learning of classmates
- Willing to struggle with uncertainty
- Enjoy challenges

### Goal for Content Area

- Make reasoned predictions
- Use prior knowledge to solve challenging problems
- Use science journals to reflect on and revise ideas

### Goal for Research Lesson

- Notice that a mathematical pattern can make it easy to solve problems
- Realize how the concepts of chance and probability apply to inheritance and evolution
- Discover that all visible objects reflect some light

### Lesson Rationale

Why did you choose to focus on this topic? For example, what do you notice about students' current understanding that led you to be interested in this topic? The lesson rationale helps the reader understand the journey that led your group to choose this topic and lesson design.

### How Does Student Understanding of This Topic Develop?

What is the trajectory of learning for this topic? U.S. educators often think of lesson study as focusing on a single lesson but, in fact, it focuses on the whole unit, even though only one lesson is typically observed. The teaching-learning plan explains how the research lesson fits within the unit—for example, whether the primary function of the lesson is to motivate students to study the topic in subsequent lessons, to help students learn a new concept, or to consolidate and apply prior learning. The teaching-learning plan also notes how the research lesson topic connects with material taught in prior or subsequent years of schooling.

*Lesson Design*

The following questions may be helpful as you plan the research lesson.

- What do students currently understand about this topic?
- What do we want them to understand at the end of the lesson and unit?
- What is the sequence of experiences and questions that will propel students from their initial understanding to the desired understanding?
- What kind of thinking, problems, and misconceptions will arise?
- What will make this lesson motivating and meaningful for students?
- What evidence should we gather and discuss about student learning, motivation, and behavior?

As shown in figure 5.5, the plan for the lesson is usually written out in three or four parallel columns that contain:

- The questions, problems, and activities to be posed by the teacher teaching the lesson
- The anticipated student responses
- The teacher's planned responses to the students and things for the teacher to remember
- Points for observers to notice during the lesson

*Student Learning Activities*

The left-hand column of the teaching-learning plan lists the major activities of the lesson and the time allocated to each activity. Each problem or major question to be posed to students is noted here. It is worth thinking through the wording and content of these questions precisely, since some small differences in task design and wording turn out to be important (for an example, see the *How Many Seats?* lesson study cycle [C. Lewis et al. 2009; Mills College Lesson Study Group 2005]).

*What Might Help Your Group Anticipate Student Thinking?*

Teacher candidates report that anticipating student thinking is the hardest part of lesson plan development as exemplified by this quote from a teacher candidate:

You have to constantly be putting yourself in their shoes and you know, it is tough. I like to think my lesson will go step 1, 2, 3, 4 and wrap up. Sometimes, I think, well maybe they need to know more about the concepts prior to step 1 or, they may come up with answers and more questions and we will spend three days immersed in step 2. I just don't know what they will come up with. I mean [I am] teaching today without really knowing where the next lesson will need to start.[5]

Several experiences will help you build your capacity to anticipate student thinking.

- Individually solve the problems or do the tasks intended for students, and share and discuss your work within your lesson study group, focusing on how different members of your lesson study group thought about the task and what you found challenging or interesting.
- Have one member microteach a lesson to other lesson study team members, and try out the lesson tasks yourselves as if you were the students, using your own and colleagues' solutions to expand your thinking about possible student responses.
- Try the task on an outside sample of students and bring their responses back to the group to discuss.
- Consult research and knowledgeable others (faculty, supervisors, mentor teachers) to get their ideas about student thinking and challenges.

### Points to Notice

The column of "points to notice" alerts observers about what to look for as they are observing each stage of the lesson. This is what your outside observers and your team are looking for in terms of evidence of how your students are learning. It is here, for example, your observers are cued to notice whether students are eager or bored to investigate a problem, what models they draw, how peer interactions influence student thinking, whether particular misconceptions surface, what prior knowledge students draw upon, and how new ideas spread within the classroom.

### Data Collection Points

What data will tell you how the students are grappling with the major ideas of your lesson? In addition to the points to notice described above, members of your team usually have specific data-collection assignments that follow from your research theme and goals. For example, teacher candidates at Mills College assigned observers to look for evidence of student engagement, persistence, and teamwork during a physics research lesson. Some observers were asked to collect data on student facial expressions and comments during individual and group work at designated lab stations. Other observers collected verbatim data on the use of academic language in student conversations and in conversations with the teacher. Team members were interested in the participation of female students in physics, and so they collected data on gender differences in task completion and student questions to the teacher.

Since these teacher candidates had designed their lesson to emphasize teamwork, they also kept narrative notes focused on the nature of communication and collaboration between students of different races and ethnicities when students were asked to join with four classmates to discuss their findings. Observers noted which learning structures supported communication within groups and at what point lesson collaboration appeared to wane or bog down.

Supports for data collection may include such things as the seating chart, station assignments for group work, checklists for noting highlights, and features of student work or forms to collect other relevant data of interest to your lesson study group. Your outside observers may also be given specific assignments.

If you will be videotaping your research lesson, think about where you want the camera to be and how it will be managed. If feasible, you may want to have a stationary camera focused on the teacher and a roving camera that follows student action. While you may be tempted to cover the entire room and all the students in your data collection, it is usually most valuable to focus on one or two students during the entire lesson so that you can document the entire lesson from their perspective, including what stimulated (or provided a barrier) to their learning.

Other important data include student work and journal entries that can be collected and examined during the post-lesson discussion and subsequently returned to students. Some lesson study groups like to build in five minutes at the end of the lesson for observers to interview the particular students they observed, in order to clarify or provide additional information on what students were thinking and what they think they learned from the lesson.

As you plan the research lesson, avoid the temptation to micromanage each move and comment of the lesson instructor. Although your group members may find it more comfortable to plan teacher moves than to deeply explore the disciplinary content, studying the content and curriculum is likely to support a more solid foundation for lesson design. If a lesson element is likely to affect students' understanding and response to the lesson task in important ways, then it is probably legitimate territory for group discussion.

Problem wording and content, choice of manipulatives, and design of graphic organizers and worksheets are all examples of lesson elements that may affect student learning. On the other hand, decisions such as whether to have a discussion at desks or gathered on the rug may best be left to the instructor, unless someone makes the case that these relate to the aspects of student learning under study by the group—for example, that it is important to be at desks so that students can record their thinking in notebooks.

A teaching-learning plan for lesson study differs from lesson plans familiar to many of us in several ways. It anticipates student thinking and how various types of student thinking will be used rather than simply laying out what the teacher will do and say. This is not surprising because the Japanese word for *lesson* (*jugyou*) in "lesson study" could equally well be translated as *instruction* and always refers to *live* instruction, not to a lesson captured on paper. This differs from the English term *lesson*, which is sometimes used interchangeably with *lesson plan*. (For example, you might hand a colleague a piece of paper and say, "Please take a look at this lesson," but the term *jugyou* could not be used in this way.)

So lesson study is not just learning about lesson design but also learning about the whole process of instruction: about student thinking and development, about subject matter, and about the interactions between the two.

Second, the teaching-learning plan is not just about a single lesson but also about how that lesson sits within a long-term trajectory of the subject matter and of student learning and development. The research lesson is important not just as an end in itself but also as a window on the goals expressed in your research theme and how you can promote them in your daily teaching.

The teaching-learning plan for lesson study embodies both long-term goals for teaching (in the form of the research theme) and hypotheses about how instruction supports those long-term goals (in the lesson rationale). It summarizes information from the first three phases of the action-research cycle described in chapter 1: issue identification, data collection, and action planning; however, at this stage, the data collected is just any preliminary information on student learning and information gathered from existing research, curricular materials, and lesson study participants' solution of the tasks. In the next phase, participants will activate the plan, gather data, and assess what has been learned, the final three phases of action research described in chapter 1.

## Phase 4: Conduct the Research Lesson

A protocol for observing the research lesson and conducting the post-lesson discussion is included in figure 5.6. This protocol is critical to successful lesson study work, because the observation and discussion expected of lesson study participants is likely to be quite different from that expected in many other contexts familiar to teachers and teacher candidates. The

**Observation of research lesson**
1. Do not help students or interfere in other ways with the lesson (such as blocking students' view of the board or teacher during teaching segments).
2. Respect the teaching process: refrain from side conversations; silence phones; stay for the entire lesson and post-lesson discussion.
3. Carefully read the teaching-learning plan and collect data requested by the lesson planning team; remember the focus is on student learning and what supported it (or provided barriers).

**Discussion of Research Lesson**
**1. The Instructor's Reflections**
The instructor describes the aims for today's lesson, comments on what went well and on any difficulties, and reflects on what was learned in planning and conducting today's lesson. (5 minutes or less.)

**2. Background Information from the Lesson Study Group Members**
The lesson study team members explain their goals for students (both lesson goals and long-term goals) and why they designed the lesson (and unit) as they did. They describe what they learned and any changes made to the lesson design over time.

**3. Presentation and Discussion of Data from the Research Lesson**
Lesson study team members (followed by observers, if any) present data from their observations. The data may include student work, a record of questions by the teacher and/or students, narrative records of all activities by particular children or small groups, record of the blackboard, etc., that have been agreed upon in advance. What do the data suggest about the students' progress on the lesson goals and goals for long-term development?

**4. General Discussion**
A brief free discussion period, facilitated by a moderator, may be provided. The focus is on student learning and development, and on how specific elements of lesson design promoted these. The moderator may designate particular themes for discussion, so that there is ordered discussion of key issues, rather than a free for all. Comments of a sensitive nature may be conveyed privately at a later time.

**5. Outside Commentator (optional)**
An invited outside commentator may discuss the lesson's relation to key subject matter issues.

**6. Thanks**
Be sure to thank publicly the instructor, planners, and attendees for their work to improve instruction.

Figure 5.6.   Research Lesson: Protocol for Observation and Discussion

team members—except for the designated teacher of the research lesson—are in the classroom to observe, not to help or interact with the students (unless you have decided on brief interviews following the lesson).

Observations should focus on student thinking and learning, not on the teacher, with a particular emphasis on the factors that supported or hindered student learning. Be sure to let the students know in advance that additional adults will be visiting and will be there to study the lesson and learn from it, not to help the students. (Otherwise, students may think they've encountered an exceptionally unhelpful group of adults!) Students should also be told in advance that adults will be listening in on group discussions and looking at student work in order to improve the lesson—*not* to evaluate the students. In Oakland, teacher candidates have found it useful to preface the research lesson by telling students: "Thank you, for helping us get smarter about teaching" (Baker 2007). It is important that your team and any invited guests are all familiar with the protocol for lesson observation.

Document the research lesson in as many ways as you can conveniently manage: videotape, audiotape, still photography, student work, and (always) careful narrative observation notes by every observer. These data will provide the basis for your post-lesson discussion of student learning.

### Phase 5: Post-Lesson Discussion and Reflection

Figure 5.6 provides a protocol for discussion of the research lesson. Once again, all participants should be familiar with it. It is good to have a facilitator hand out and go over the protocol before the discussion begins and for all to adhere to it. If time permits, give participants twenty minutes or so to reflect quietly, organize their observational notes, and examine student work or artifacts from the lesson before starting the post-lesson discussion.

The discussion begins with a brief reflection by the instructor who taught the lesson, and continues with reports from each observer, focusing on the data they collected and its implications for the group's questions of interest. The focus is on reporting data, not on evaluative comments or inferences. Some lesson study teams organize data reporting around their key questions, for example, what did our observations tell us about students' use of primary source documents (editing strategies, use of prior knowledge, etc.)? How did key elements of the lesson (e.g., the manipulatives, models, problems) support or hinder student learning? This may help to avoid "bed-to-bed" stories which describe everything students did but do not relate it to the questions of interest to the group. Packets of colored sticky notes may be helpful for marking student work or observation notes related to particular questions of interest to the group.

A final commentator helps to summarize key points from the observations and to connect the lesson and discussion to important issues in the field. Attention to protocol elements, such as remembering to thank the teacher who taught the lesson, will help build the climate for continued collaborative work. Not everything needs to be said in the post-lesson discussion, and comments of a personal nature are best conveyed at another time. The post-lesson discussion often naturally suggests ways that the lesson might be revised, and participants will want to revise and re-teach it in another classroom if time permits. Typically, the revision of the lesson for re-teaching takes much less time than the original planning of the lesson.

Teachers and teacher candidates have found it useful to consolidate their learning from the entire cycle by writing an end of cycle reflection that includes what they learned about content, student learning, and working with colleagues in this action research effort. You can find a PowerPoint template to help you summarize your learning and present it to others at www.lessonresearch.net. Or the reflection questions at the close of this chapter may be helpful.

One difference between lesson study and some other forms of research is that lesson study is designed to develop not just knowledge that can be disseminated in the form of research articles or lesson plans but also to develop the "knowers" themselves. Successful lesson study should develop teachers' knowledge of content, pedagogy, and students, including knowledge that can be used in the "hot action" of classroom instruction (C. Lewis et al. 2009; C. Lewis, Perry, Hurd, & O'Connell 2006).

Successful lesson study should also develop productive dispositions toward practice, identity as learners, and relationships with colleagues (C. Lewis 2009). The following reflection questions may help you consider how lesson study contributed to your knowledge and development. Typically, lesson study builds impact as it is practiced over time (Perry & Lewis 2008). So the following questions may also enable you to identify aspects of your lesson study work you want to improve over time.

What did we learn from this lesson study cycle:

- About the subject matter?
- About teaching?
- About student learning?
- About working within a community of teachers?

What insights did we gain from this lesson study cycle about productive habits in our learning practices as teachers, such as:

- Anticipation of student thinking?
- Study and comparison of curriculum?

- Drawing on outside knowledge resources (research, subject matter specialists, etc.)?
- Careful observation of student learning?

## QUESTIONS FOR REVIEW AND REFLECTION

1. How does lesson study relate to the action research framework described in chapter 1?
2. How might lesson study influence teachers and the knowledge base for teaching?
3. Take a lesson familiar to you and select a focus for the observation and post-lesson discussion in lesson study, explaining why you chose it.
4. Describe the cycle of inquiry that occurs within lesson study.
5. How does the teaching-learning plan differ from lesson plans familiar to you?

## NOTES

1. This material is based upon work supported by the National Science Foundation under Grant No. 0207259 and DRL–0633945. Any opinions, findings, and conclusions or recommendations expressed in this material are those of the author(s) and do not necessarily reflect the views of the National Science Foundation. We wish to acknowledge the contributions of Rebecca Perry and Jackie Hurd to the ideas in this chapter.

2. Class discussion comment by student teacher, Mills College class, Oakland, California.

3. Class discussion comment by student teacher, 2004, Mills College class, Oakland, California.

4. Class discussion comment by student teacher, 2002, Mills College class, Oakland, California.

5. Class discussion comment by student teacher, 2003, Mills College class, Oakland, California.

## REFERENCES

Baker, E. (2007). *Lesson study in the pre-service setting.* Unpublished doctoral dissertation. Mills College, Oakland, CA.

Cossey, R., & Tucher, P. (2005). Teaching to collaborate, collaborating to teach. *Teaching as principles practice: Managing complexity for social justice.* Thousand Oaks, CA: Sage Publications.

Finken, T., Matthews, M., Hlas, C., & Schmidt, J. (2004). *Integrating lesson study for pre-service and in-service teachers.* Paper presented at the poster session of the National Council of Teachers of Mathematics (NCTM).

Hiebert, J., Morris, A. K., & Glass, B. (2003). Learning to learn to teach: An "experiment" model for teaching and teacher preparation in mathematics. *Journal of Mathematics Teacher Education, 6*(3), 201–22.

Hurd, J., & Licciardo-Musso, L. (2005). Lesson study: Teacher led professional development in literacy instruction. *Language Arts, 82*(5), 388–95.

Lewis, C. (2000). *Lesson study: The core of Japanese professional development.* Paper presented at the American Educational Research Association.

Lewis, C. (2002). *Lesson study: A handbook of teacher-led instructional change.* Philadelphia: Research for Better Schools.

Lewis, C. (2009). What is the nature of knowledge development in lesson study? *Educational Action Research, 17*(1), 95–110.

Lewis, C., Perry, R., & Hurd, J. (2009). Improving mathematics instruction through lesson study: A theoretical model and North American case. *Journal of Mathematics Teacher Education, 12*(4), 285–304.

Lewis, C., Perry, R., Hurd, J., & O'Connell, M. P. (2006). Lesson study comes of age in North America. *Phi Delta Kappan, December,* 273–81.

Lewis, C., & Tsuchida, I. (1997). Planned educational change in Japan: The case of elementary science instruction. *Journal of Educational Policy, 12*(5), 313–31.

Lewis, J. (2007). *Teaching as invisible work.* Unpublished doctoral dissertation, University of Michigan.

Mills College Lesson Study Group (2000). *Can you lift 100 kilograms?* [DVD]. Oakland, CA: Mills College Lesson Study Group.

Mills College Lesson Study Group (2005). *How many seats? Excerpts of a lesson study cycle.* [DVD]. Oakland, CA: Mills College Lesson Study Group.

Ogden, N., Perkins, C., & Donahue, D. M. (2008). Not a peculiar institution: Challenging students' assumptions about slavery in U.S. history. *History Teacher, 41*(4), 469–88.

Perry, R., & Lewis, C. (2008). What is successful adaptation of lesson study in the U.S.? *Journal of Educational Change, 10*(4), 365–91.

Perry, R., Tucher, P., & Lewis, C. (2003). *Lesson study in pre-service education, Mills College.* Paper presented at the annual meeting of the American Education Research Association, Chicago, IL.

Pesick, S. (2005). "Lesson study" and the teaching of American history: Connecting professional development and classroom practice. *Social Studies Review, California Council for the Social Studies* (Spring).

Shimizu, Y. (2002). *Sharing a new approach to teaching mathematics with the teachers from outside the school: The role of lesson study at "Fuzoku" schools.* Paper presented at the U.S.–Japan Cross Cultural Seminar on the Professionalization of Teachers Through Lesson Study, Park City, UT.

Stigler, J. W., & Hiebert, J. (1999). *The teaching gap: Best ideas from the world's teachers for improving education in the classroom.* New York: Summit Books.

Takahashi, A. (2000). Current trends and issues in lesson study in Japan and the United States. *Journal of Japan Society of Mathematical Education, 82*(no. 12: 49–6), 15–21.

Taylor, A., & Puchner, L. (2003). Learning from lesson study in Illinois. *Illinois Mathematics Teacher, 54*(1), 20–25.

Wang-Iverson, P., & Yoshida, M. (2005). *Building our understanding of lesson study.* Philadelphia: Research for Better Schools.

## APPENDIX A. SAMPLE SCHEDULE FOR INTEGRATION OF LESSON STUDY IN PRESERVICE COURSE

| | |
|---|---|
| One class session | Build shared understanding of lesson study<br>In preparation read:<br>Chapter 7, The Teaching Gap (Stigler & Hiebert 1999)<br>Pelton, Chapter 1, "An Introduction to Action Research";<br>Lesson Study Handbook (Lewis 2002)<br>Observe video: *Can you Lift One Hundred Kilograms?* (Mills College, 2000)<br>Discuss: What are the key elements of lesson study? How do teachers learn during lesson study? |
| One class session | Choose Roles (i.e. facilitator; notetaker; time keeper;)<br>Develop Group Norms;<br>Consider Long-Term Goals: See Figure 5.4 "Developing the Research Theme for Lesson Study"<br>Reference Materials: |
| As time permits (3-5 sessions) | Determine your content focus and begin your research, study, and planning by solving tasks, anticipating student thinking, sharing and discussing task responses, comparing curricula, studying research.<br>Consider possible dates and classes for research lesson.<br>Contact outside observers and knowledgable others to synchronize schedules. |
| One class session | Research Lesson |
| Immediately following research lesson; one additional class if available | Post-lesson discussion of the Research Lesson.<br>Consolidate and summarize learning on lesson study as a form of Action Research. |

# 6

---

# Teacher Work Sample Methodology as a Frame for Action Research

*Marie LeJeune, PhD, Assistant Professor, Division of Teacher Education, Western Oregon University*

*Tracy Smiles, PhD, Assistant Professor, Division of Teacher Education, Western Oregon University*

*Steve Wojcikiewicz, PhD, Assistant Professor, Division of Teacher Education, Western Oregon University*

*Mark Girod, PhD, Associate Professor, Chair, Division of Teacher Education, Western Oregon University*

## INTRODUCTION

Since there is no one "right" way to carry out action research, it can be quite challenging to choose among the different methodologies that may fit with the particular context and focus of your inquiry (Goswami, Lewis, Rutherford, & Waff 2009). In this chapter, teacher work sample methodology (TWSM), an increasingly popular method of preparing and assessing teachers, is presented as a potential frame for your action research project.

We will discuss both TWSM (the process or method of engaging in this sort of research) and the actual TWS (the physical product that is created during the process) as well as how this process embodies the principles of action research to create a deeply thoughtful inquiry study.

Although there are multiple approaches to action research, the theoretical underpinnings of all of them center on the belief that teachers can use systematic examination of practice to open up powerful opportunities for the improvement of both teaching and learning. Since teacher work sample methodology is data driven, reflective, and centered around the value of connecting teaching to student learning, it is by nature a highly effective form of action research. This chapter will provide descriptions, examples, and guidelines for the use of teacher work sample methodology, all geared to help you engage in action research that examines possible ways in which teaching is connected to learning

## CHAPTER OBJECTIVES

By the time you finish reading and thinking about this chapter you will be able to:

- Define work sample methodology
- List the basic steps and features of TWSM
- Describe the rationale for the use of teacher work sample methodology in action research
- Employ TWSM as an effective form of action research to create meaningful experience of teacher inquiry.

## WHY TEACHER WORK
## SAMPLE METHODOLOGY?

Teacher work sample methodology (TWSM) is a performance-assessment process that is built around the idea of linking teacher performance to student learning (Girod 2008; Schalock & Myton 2002). TWSM aims to make this link by asking teacher candidates like you to systematically document, examine, analyze, and reflect upon their own teaching practices and student outcomes. While planning, preparing, conducting, and reflecting upon the process of a teacher work sample (TWS), candidates are essentially seeking to understand how well students learned what they intended to teach.

TWSM includes components (description of the setting, assessments, lesson plans, etc.) that provide evidence that candidates can employ the conceptual skills needed for effective teaching (analysis of context, selection of content and pedagogy, etc.). Teacher work samples demonstrate that candidates can connect their actions as teachers to the learning of their students (M. Girod 2008).

Teacher work sample methodology represents a leap forward in how we think about the relationship between teacher performance and student learning. While it may not seem strange to you, a teacher candidate in the twenty-first century, the idea of linking teaching to learning was quite revolutionary when TWSM was first developed more than twenty years ago.

Prior to the development of TWSM, teachers were assumed to be qualified to enter the classroom upon completion of their courses and field experiences. When these "qualified" teachers were teaching, it was assumed that student learning was a result (Cochran-Smith 2008; Grossman 2008; Schalock & Myton 1988). The original developers of TWSM sought to examine these assumptions. They wondered if they could make student learning the centerpiece of teacher evaluation and sought ways to change "the design of a teacher's work" (Schalock, Shalock, & Girod 1997, p. 19), pushing teachers to take their teaching contexts into consideration when planning, through the alignment of objectives, instruction, and assessments.

The framework of TWSM is well aligned with current trends in the field of teacher education. As you may already know, there is a greater emphasis being placed on data-driven and outcome-based accountability in the field of education, perhaps more than ever before (Cochran-Smith 2006; 2008), and TWSM supports the growing desire to assess teacher performance in these ways (Schalock & Myton 2002). Furthermore, while past investigations (Coleman et al. 1966) found little evidence that teachers play a central role in student achievement, more recent work has confirmed the long-held belief that creative, innovative, caring teachers make a difference in the lives and learning of children (Gelberg 2007; Nieto 2005; National Commission on Teaching and America's Future 1996).

TWSM is one way that such a difference, in the form of student learning, might be measured and documented, bringing TWSM in line with another current goal of university-based teacher preparation programs: the desire to link evidence from candidates, candidate learning, candidate practices, contextual factors, and P–12 student learning (Cochran-Smith 2005b; Fredman 2004; G. Girod 2002; M. Girod 2008). Because of the matches between TWSM and these trends, this methodology is growing in popularity today and is currently required for licensure in eight states.

If you are wondering what this has to do with you, the aspiring action researcher, the answer is this: because the priorities and design of teacher work sample methodology is well suited for use in framing and carrying out action research projects while simultaneously meeting the stringent criteria for providing evidence in a teacher candidate's competency and preparedness to teach.

Teacher work sampling builds upon the same primary question that guides action research as noted in the first chapter of this book: "How well are my students learning what I intend to teach?" Additionally, TWSM fits with both the "action" and the "research" aspects of action research. TWSM has proven to be a valid measure of the tasks that teachers carry out every day (Denner, Norman, Salzman, & Pankratz 2003; Denner, Salzman, & Bangert 2001), and seeks to build up a vision of teaching that is reflective and recursive. Because TWSM is a data-driven system, it also fits well with the demands you will experience as a teacher in the current climate of accountability and evidence. Finally, TWSM provides a proven framework for teacher inquiry, a framework that you can use to structure an action research project specific to your context and your needs.

## THE BASIC FRAMEWORK OF TEACHER
## WORK SAMPLE METHODOLOGY

A good first step in considering the use of TWSM as a frame for approaching an action research project is to examine the components included in typical applications of TWSM. Teacher work sample methodology may look different depending on the purpose of the inquiry and/or specific institutional requirements, but in general they involve teacher candidates learning to establish links between teaching and learning by following a process of well-aligned planning, instruction, and assessment. This process yields a product known as a *teacher work sample*, a product which, by and large, includes the following sections (Girod 2008):

1. *setting description*—a thorough description of the setting at the community, school, and classroom levels
2. *rationale and goals or objectives*—a discussion of content selection, pedagogical choices, and student-learning goals
3. *lesson plans*—lessons as illustrations selection choices
4. *assessment plan*—preparation of pre-, post-, and formative assessments including discussions of alignment, validity, and reliability
5. *data analysis*—representation of learning-gain data by objective, including individuals and groups, clearly represented and appropriately interpreted
6. *reflective essay*—an analysis of effectiveness of teaching, set in terms of student learning, including critiques of unit implementation and ideas for the future

While these sections make up the physical end-product that is called a *teacher work sample*, it is important for you to keep in mind that the construction of a work sample is not in and of itself the point of the TWSM process. A teacher work sample is, after all, a "sample" of "teacher's work."

Undergirding the teacher work sample and its components is a series of skills. Each of these skills must be developed during teacher-preparation experiences, documented through elements of performance assessment, and woven together in real-world settings. It is important to distinguish between the underlying conceptual skillfulness being developed and the components of the teacher work sample. The teacher work sample itself, the final product, should really be viewed as a set of evidence that teacher candidates have learned to successfully link their work as teachers to the learning of P–12 students. This "connecting of teaching and learning" (G. Girod 2002) is accomplished as teacher candidates become proficient in the implementation of seven critical skills for effective teachers:

1. *analysis of context*—effective teachers examine carefully the setting in which they will be teaching including the constraints and affordances within the system as well as the strengths, weaknesses, prior knowledge, experiences, and interests of the students
2. *selection of outcomes*—effective teachers select outcomes that are valuable and aligned with the needs of the learners
3. *selection of pedagogy*—effective teachers select pedagogical strategies that make sense given the outcomes and context
4. *use sound assessment practices*—effective teachers design valid and reliable assessment systems
5. *data analysis*—effective teachers use assessment to support student learning by providing accurate and timely feedback on student progress toward outcomes
6. *reflection*—effective teachers are able to reflect on the processes of teaching and learning in ways that help them diagnose student learning and their own professional development needs
7. *alignment*—effective teachers structure this entire process in ways that align the demands of context, content, pedagogy, and assessment to maximize student learning. Teacher candidates demonstrate each of these conceptual understandings through the preparation of a teacher work sample.

Table 6.1 summarizes the connections between the conceptual skills underlying the creation of a teacher work sample and components that provide evidence of these skills (M. Girod 2008). Figure 6.1. links the stages of action research to individual components of the TWS.

## WORK SAMPLE METHODOLOGY AS
## A FORM OF ACTION RESEARCH

Now that we've explored TWSM and its components and rationale, let's look at how the action research principles work to create a stronger, more reflective piece of teacher research that combines the principles of both TWSM and action research. Drawing upon the Five Step Action Research Process introduced in chapter 1, we'll examine how the components and skills of TWSM have confluence with the steps and skills involved in the action research process. To review, the five steps integral to the action research process are (1) issue identification, (2) data collection, (3) action planning,

**Table 6.1. Conceptual skills underlying the components of a teacher work sample**

| Conceptual skill | Description | Work sample component | Description |
|---|---|---|---|
| Analysis of context | Candidates must be proficient in analysis of the context in which teaching and learning will occur with a particular attention toward qualities, experiences, dispositions, circumstances, or other factors that may have an impact on teaching and learning. | Setting description | Candidates write a thorough description of the setting at the community, school, and classroom levels. Opportunities abound for the kinds of data to include, but the consequences on teaching and learning must always be considered. |
| Selection of content | Candidates must be proficient in selection of content that is important, powerful, and useful in the lives and estimation of students, community, and state and national standards. | Rationale and goals/ objectives | Candidates offer a discussion of content selection choices and demonstration of alignment between content selected and standards governing that content and context. This is commonly done in a table or listing of standards and goals/objectives. |
| Selection of pedagogy | Candidates must be proficient in the selection of pedagogy that is best aligned with the context, content, and student prior knowledge making learning most likely to occur efficiently and deeply. | Lesson plans | Candidates design lessons as illustrations of these selection judgments. |
| Assessment | Candidates must be proficient in the design of measures and experiences to collect information about student prior knowledge related to learning outcomes selected, "in-flight" learning, and learning at the conclusion of a unit of instruction. | Assessment plan including pre-, post-, and formative tests | Candidates must offer clear and compelling logic for structuring assessment procedures in the manner chosen, illustrate how assessment items are aligned with goals and objectives (commonly through a table of specifications), and defend the assessments themselves as valid and reliable measures of student learning. |

| | | | |
|---|---|---|---|
| Data analysis | Candidates must be proficient in the analysis of many kinds of data including prior to, during, and after instruction. This analysis must examine data in aggregate as well as disaggregated across groups such as students with special needs, ELL's, students living in poverty, and minority students. | Data analysis | Candidates must represent various "cuts" on learning-gain data, at the individual objective level, for both individuals and groups. These data should be clearly represented and discussed appropriately. |
| Reflective analysis | Candidates must be proficient in reflecting on their work as teacher, the progress and engagement of their students, and the interaction and alignment between setting, content, pedagogy, and assessment. Reflection is a central element of the work sample and can be viewed as an illustration of reflective capacity. | Reflective essay | Though reflection is critical to the completion of an exemplary work sample, the clearest evidence of this reflection is found at the end of the work sample in the reflective essay. In this, candidates write in analysis of their effectiveness in helping all students reach the goals and objectives as defined. Additionally, candidates should reflect on their future professional needs. |
| Alignment | Likely the most critical concept of all, candidates must be proficient in aligning assessment procedures, learning experiences, goals and objectives, and contextual factors in a way that is most conducive to learning. There ought to be clear and compelling logic for the decisions made by the candidate; this is the essence of evidence-based decision making. | No single representation | Alignment is something that must be inferred in a teacher work sample. There is no section in a work sample that describes alignment decisions though a thoughtfully constructed one might allude to alignment decisions made throughout all the components. For example, a well-constructed work sample would offer a description of the instructional strategies chosen and how they make best sense in light of the context, the content, and the goals and objectives pursued. |

|  | Issue Identification | Data Collection | Action Planning | Plan Activation | Outcome Assessment |
|---|---|---|---|---|---|
| Setting | X |  | X |  |  |
| Rationale/Goals and Objectives | X |  | X |  |  |
| Lesson Plans |  | X | X | X |  |
| Assessment Plan |  | X | X | X |  |
| Data Analysis |  | X |  |  | X |
| Reflective Essay |  |  |  |  | X |

**Figure 6.1.   Intersections of Work Sample Components and Action Research Steps**

(4) plan activation, and (5) outcome assessment. We'll begin with issue identification.

### TWS and Issue Identification

Generally within action research, the researcher—the teacher—identifies an issue or question they want to examine within their own practice and setting. These questions often arise from areas we want to improve in our own practice or new pedagogies or content we'd like to explore with students, and so on. These often come from what we might call our *wonderings* about teaching and student learning (Hubbard & Powers 2003).

For those of you who are beginning to embark upon the process of the TWS or those of you have completed a TWS in the past, you may wonder how issue identification connects to TWS methodology. Scheduling demands and course content in the classroom (as well as the preferences of mentor or coordinating teachers) often dictate what subject or unit of study the TWS will cover. Many student teachers are flatly told that their work sample must cover a certain topic—for example, the three branches of government or *Of Mice and Men* or plate tectonics. Where then do teacher candidates have room to explore and identify issues that they find compelling and important through the TWS?

Despite the fact that some teacher candidates receive little input into the topic of their TWS, this does not mean that there is not a huge amount of room for issue identification and a focus on true action research through the TWS. In fact, the TWS can offer a way for a teacher candidate to unearth the infinite possibilities for action research because of its focus on connecting teaching and learning, which is at the heart of what we do as teachers.

Although the teacher candidate may not always have complete input on the topic of the TWS, they do (and must have) control over the design and implementation of the TWS itself, which provides a myriad of opportunities to thoughtfully reflect upon and develop issues of importance within both the teacher's own practice and students' learning to systematically examine. Teacher candidates systematically study and describe the setting of their school and classroom community. They also utilize state and national professional and academic standards to develop goals and objectives for student learning.

Throughout the construction of the TWS, you will be responsible for designing the content, goals and objectives, and pedagogy for your instruction. Teacher candidates additionally must develop assessment tools to examine students' prior knowledge and the knowledge gained through the teaching of the TWS. All of these (and other) steps support a systematic examination of practice—a key component of action research.

Let's consider the three topics of study we already mentioned: the three branches of government, *Of Mice and Men,* and plate tectonics.

Although TWSM requires teacher candidates to systematically examine the connection between their teaching and student learning, this often takes place through an examination of data around established goals and objectives. This is valuable, crucial data for you as a developing teacher. We'd like to expand upon this frame and consider how you, as a novice teacher and a beginning action researcher, might develop a "wondering" or a research question within the context of your TWS. To do this, we'll examine three crucial criteria within any research situation—participants (for you this will be your students), methodology (for you this will be your pedagogy and teaching using various research-based strategies), and finally the results (your students' learning outcomes).

The following list illustrates potential questions or issues that could be systematically examined within the work sample using this proposed three part framework for devising a research question. These example questions consider the following: learners (Who are the students who will benefit from the study? Again, these are your participants, but as TWSM focuses on student learning, we believe learners may be a more helpful term for you as you explore your TWS as an action research endeavor ), teaching strategy (What are the teaching strategies to achieve these outcomes? This is your methodology—the strategies and pedagogical decisions you will employ while teaching your work sample), and learning outcomes (What are the learning outcomes discovered? These are your results.) (Shambaugh & Webb-Dempsey 2008). The following are examples of action research questions specific to units of study:

- How does a combination of direct instruction and cooperative work groups (strategy) help fourth grade students (students) learn the three branches of government (content)?

- In what ways do literature circles (strategy) help tenth grade students (students) comprehend and interpret *Of Mice and Men* (content)?
- In what ways do graphic organizers (strategy) help seventh grade ESOL students (students) represent their understanding of earth science principles (content)?

These questions focus on the connection between teaching and student learning and are generative in their potential to lead the action researcher in expanding their understanding of student experience and growth, pedagogy and best practice, and curricula development.

After key questions and/or issues are identified, the next step is to begin considering what kinds of data sources can be collected and analyzed to address the focus of the inquiry. Following is a discussion of data collection and the TWS.

### TWS and Data Collection

Pelton asserts in chapter 1 that the data we collect are important factors in the decisions we make. The challenge, however, for most teacher researchers is in the process of organizing and making use of the information they gather. This is particularly so because as teachers we are immersed every day in endless possibilities for data sources: our own informal observations of student behavior, students' written and spoken comments, assessment data (both formative and summative) to include classroom assignments, quizzes, projects, and so forth. A potential strength of the methodology behind the TWS is that it can provide an organizational frame for supporting a teacher researcher in focusing on the kinds of data that will provide factual and useful information to examine the issue or research question identified.

When examining the issue of data collection, it is clear that the TWS requires a systematic gathering and documentation of various data. When constructing the setting of the TWS, students must draw upon both formal and informal data sources about the geographic, social, economic, and cultural factors that influence the classroom and larger community in which the study (the TWS) takes place.

A key component of the TWS also requires teacher candidates to gather important data such as pre-assessment data, formative assessment data, and summative assessment data. In addition, daily observations and reflections at the end of each teaching day provide a thoughtful, qualitative description of the ongoing study through the teacher candidate creating what is essentially a short analytic memo (Jessop & Penney 1999) in which they record their daily reflections about teaching and learning. All of these are valuable data that are essential to the TWS and also, if used properly, can allow you to frame your TWS as an action research project.

Although data collection is an essential part of TWS, when approaching the TWS from an action research mindset, you will want to be deliberate and conscientious about verifying that the types of data you are gathering are sufficient to answer your research question. You may want to collect a few additional pieces of data during the teaching of your TWS—such as an informal interview with a student or a questionnaire about students' attitudes about the subject being taught. Again, the types of data gathered depend upon the question itself. Figure 6.2. provides a revisit of our examples and explores what sort of data a teacher candidate might want to collect, depending upon their research question.

You will find that figure 6.2 illustrates how particular data sources can purposefully address specific kinds of questions and issues. When questions have been proposed and potential data sources identified, you are ready to create a plan that addresses the issue you are going to explore through your TWS.

| Guiding Question | Data Sources |
| --- | --- |
| How does a combination of direct instruction and cooperative work groups (strategy) help fourth grade students (students) learn the three branches of government (content)? | Pre and post testing, lesson plans, student produced artifacts and assignments, field notes taken while students engage in cooperative groups, an exit survey of students about their experiences in cooperative groups, etc. |
| In what ways do literature circles (strategy) help tenth grade students (student) comprehend and interpret *Of Mice and Men* (content)? | Observational field notes, student journals, written reflections/research memos, recorded discussions |
| In what ways do graphic organizers help seventh grade ELL students represent their understanding of Earth Science principles? | Students' final project, attitudinal survey given to students regarding using graphic organizers, etc. |

Pre and post-testing, student work—**records student performance**
**Lesson plans**—records teaching
**Student journals, recorded discussions**—records students' experiences and conceptual understandings
**Research memos/ written reflections**—records implementation of the plan, reflection and revision of the plan, next steps

**Figure 6.2.   Description of Data Sources**
(Figure 2. Adapted from Shambaugh & Webb-Dempsey, 2008).

## TWS and Action Planning

Action planning is central to both the TWS and action research as a whole. Continued research in teacher effectiveness (Gore & Zeichner 1991; Valli 2000) supports the huge importance of extensive planning and preparation for any teaching situation. Effective teachers, those who consistently reflect upon their own planning and teaching and students' learning outcomes have the opportunity to continually improve their practice and, in turn, increase student achievement (Darling-Hammond & Bransford 2005; Shepard 2001).

As a novice teacher, you will find that planning a thoughtful, well-scaffolded, and successful lesson plan takes a great amount of time and consideration. Luckily, lesson planning and larger planning such as TWS action research projects need not be done in isolation; there are many professional and pedagogical resources for you to draw upon when constructing your methodology.

When embarking upon action research and the TWS as a teacher candidate, you are able to draw upon helpful resources from both your university education (professors, prior coursework and readings, library resources, etc.) as well as those from your field placement (your mentor teacher's expertise, other professionals in your field placement, etc.). Although it is critical for you to design and format your own individual lesson plans, assessments, and teaching tools so that the action plan is ultimately designed by you for the particular setting of the classroom you are working in, teaching and teacher research need not be an isolated experience. Effective teachers know that collaborating with others on planning and assessment or even looking to another professional for advice and guidance can help improve practice and certainly helps us become reflective practitioners.

Referring again to one of our proposed units of study, while carrying out an action plan for TWS, a teacher might want to draw upon the following sources:

Guiding question: How does a combination of direct instruction and cooperative work groups (strategy) help fourth grade students (students) learn the three branches of government (content)?

*Possible Sources*

- *Mentor teacher*—share experiences using cooperative learning groups, knowledge of students' specific needs as learners, other resources.
- *University social studies content specialist*—share both content and pedagogical knowledge and resources, offer support in thinking through the key issues related to your questions and advice on conducting and analyzing research.

- *Professional literature such as articles and books*—provide rich descriptions from other teacher researchers and findings from research related to teaching social studies using collaborative work groups that provide direction and insight when examining your data.
- *Other teacher candidates*—offer insights into data you may not initially consider and support, while facing the teaching, researching, and writing challenges you may encounter. (You are not alone).

Now that you have collected and examined your data, read professional literature, and discussed your research with colleagues, mentors, and professors, you are ready for the critical step of activating a plan based on your new learning and understandings in order to improve the educational experiences for your students and all those served by the school community.

### TWS and Plan Activation

This step of the action research process is pretty straightforward; now is the time to put into action all that you have planned and researched. At this point you will begin to teach the lessons you've carefully planned for your TWS. A crucial component of the TWS that will support your action research agenda will be the daily lesson reflections. Taking time while your data (your actual teaching and the students' engagement in the learning process) is still fresh will allow you to record rich qualitative data such as your observations of students' behaviors, comments that students make during class, difficulties and successes you encounter in your daily teaching, and so forth. Again, this is a crucial time to take on what is referred to in chapter 1 as the reflection-in-action mindset where the actual teaching of your TWS and the creation of your reflective action research marry together to inform your practice.

Again, we'd like to examine how this might look within a TWS component, that of the daily lesson plan reflection. We've included some examples of the types of details that might strengthen a daily reflection entry and make it a valuable data source as you consider your TWS through the lens of action research.

Example Research Question: *In what ways do literature circles help tenth grade students comprehend and interpret the novel* Of Mice and Men?

Excerpt from a sample daily reflection from the above student teacher's TWS:
*Today was the first day students participated in a literature circle discussion in my class. I had students fill out a short, three-question survey about their experiences reading novels in school. I wanted to see what students had liked and*

*disliked in the past and how much experience they had with peer-led discussions rather than teacher-directed discussion. I think this will be valuable data later on.*

*Using the example from my methods professor, I modeled the process of how a literature circle works by working with a shorter piece of literature today, a poem about loneliness that I thought the kids would enjoy and that would be accessible for them to read. Then we did a trial run at a literature circle discussion based upon their response to the poem. I walked around and listened to the various groups as they discussed the poem.*

*I was happy to see most kids appear to be on task and I will be interested to see if my perceptions match up to the data I collect on students' progress. A few kids were off-task at times and I had to remind them of what the objective of the lesson was—I need to talk more to my mentor teacher about ways to help keep kids productive when they are in a small group setting.*

Let's examine what sorts of important details we notice in the above excerpt from a student's daily lesson plan reflection. First, this candidate does a good job of not only describing the events of the lesson by giving rich details as she also includes her thoughts about what happened and how this either supported her learning objectives or had opportunities for improvement. She also manages, in a very concise yet complete manner, to include details about each of the aspects of her research question—the learners, the strategies, and pedagogy she employed, and what she was beginning to observe as learning outcomes or results. She also was employing additional data collection such as the short survey to collect information to answer her research question. Finally, she shows evidence of drawing upon both her own professional knowledge as well as resources from her university education (methods course work) and her field placement (asking advice of her mentor teacher). Although this is only an example of a short excerpt from a longer overall daily reflection, it provides an example of how your daily reflections can provide valuable data as you blend action research perspectives into TWSM.

### TWS and Outcome Assessment

Outcome assessment in action research involves reflecting back upon the process you've engaged in thus far, examining your original research question, analyzing the data you've collected and attempting to synthesize what you have learned from both the process of constructing the research and the actual findings you've discerned from the data. This, again, is a process that is required for completion of the TWS. Creating a TWS involves the systematic gathering and documentation of various data (including, but not limited to, extensive assessment data) and the analysis of that data to identify learning outcomes as well as knowledge about teaching and best practice. Additionally, the TWS includes a final, holistic reflection piece that

is written in a narrative format, ideally with rich details and recommendations for future practice based upon the results gathered during the teaching
and analysis of the TWS.

Action research involves this aforementioned systematic, sustained documentation of various data sources, including options for both quantitative
(numeric and discrete) and qualitative (narrative and descriptive) data
sources. A strength of the TWS as a means of pursuing action research is
that it truly can be a mixed-methods approach to research, combining both
numeric assessment data, such as pre- and post-test results, and the rich
qualitative descriptions that are often found in pieces such as the setting
and the reflection essay.

The TWS method of action research also focuses on what teachers themselves can learn from being reflective and conscientious about planning,
practice, pedagogy, and assessment, by using the reflective essay as a crucial
piece within the research process. This is where you have the opportunity to
draw together the various threads within the TWS and your research; an exemplary TWS when used as action research will create a vivid, clear picture
into the classroom setting, the teaching that occurred, the students' learning, and the developing answers to the "wonderings" you developed within
your issue identification. This is also a vital place for you to reflect upon
what this research has meant to you, your teaching, and your thoughts for
future practice.

Again, we'd like to share some exemplary examples of how you might
utilize your reflective essay in your TWS to display the knowledge you have
learned throughout the research and teaching process:

> Example Research Question: *How does a combination of direct instruction and
> cooperative work groups help fourth grade students learn the three branches of gov-
> ernment?*

Excerpt from final reflective essay:
*Overall, I am pleased with the outcome of my unit on the three branches of
government and the amount of learning that took place with my fourth graders.
Although I was originally overwhelmed by the vast possibilities of what I could
teach about this subject and the manner in which I could help structure and design
my lessons to scaffold this information for younger students, I found that the huge
amount of planning I did prior to teaching this unit truly paid off for both myself
and my students.*

*After doing my original planning for this unit, I met with my curriculum and
assessment professor and realized that I was planning in a way that overly emphasized direct instruction. When we talked through my lessons, I realized that there
were way too many times during the unit where I was simply expecting students
to listen to me while I was delivering information through direct instruction—the
students didn't have enough opportunities to actually work actively on constructing*

*knowledge through doing. This is when I realized I needed to rethink my pedagogy and this is also where my overall research question for this project came from—this need or gap I saw in my own practice; I was planning to teach the way I'd been taught rather than the ways I had learned were more beneficial in my education classes.*

*I think I was so nervous about the vast amount of information I thought I should cover to meet the standards that I hadn't really reflected on the learning process for these nine-year-old kids. Again, I am reminded of how important not teaching and planning in isolation is; if I had not worked through the construction of my Work Sample as a process with my professor I might likely have really focused on direct instruction, which I believe from the data I have collected in this TWS illustrates that student learning would have been impacted in a negative way by this.*

*When I developed my question about involving collaborative, cooperative learning to improve student outcomes, I was able to then collect data from the activities that students engaged in cooperatively.*

*My data throughout this project shows that students often scored higher on assessments and assignments after working cooperatively with a partner or in a small group setting. In some ways this shouldn't have been such a surprise to me; after all this is exactly what I've been taught in my teacher education classes. The truth is, though, it really impacts you in a new way when you see it in your classroom with your students. I am sold—cooperative learning will be a regular part of my teaching practice. I am looking forward to reading and learning about other strategies that will help me employ cooperative engagements successfully with my elementary students.*

Again, let's debrief some of the details from this excerpt from a reflective essay written by a student working in an elementary classroom with social studies content.

First, this student does a strong job of describing process—the process by which he arrived at his research question through issue identification (realizing that he was overemphasizing direct instruction in his original lesson plan drafts), the process by which he created the lessons and also revised the lessons for his TWS, the process of working collaboratively with resources available to him (his university professor), and the process by which he then taught his actual work sample and reflected upon how it impacted the learners in his classroom.

In this short excerpt from an overall longer reflective essay, we are also able to see rich details that attend to each aspect of the action research process—issue identification (his research question), data collection (the assignments and assessments he gave in class as well as his own observations and the creation of this reflective piece itself), action planning (described here with interesting details about how he revised his plans after working collaboratively during the action planning process), plan activation (description of how he involved students in partner and small group work), and outcome assessment (acknowledgment that data analysis revealed that students showed greater learning gains after opportunities to work collaboratively with one another).

As this is just a short example illustrated as an excerpt from an overall longer reflective essay (which might run several pages), each aspect of the action research framework is ideally described in continued depth throughout the essay. Again, this reflective essay itself is a valuable means of creating a rich piece of descriptive, qualitative data that serves as one important aspect of outcome assessment in the action research process and framework.

## CONCLUSION: TWS AS ACTION RESEARCH— *A REFLECTION-IN-ACTION MINDSET*

Although there is a clear connection between TWS and the process of action research, it is crucial to remember that neither TWS or action research (nor teaching itself) are linear processes in which we complete tasks on a to-do list. Instead, this is a recursive, spiraling process in which we may go back and forth between the various stages. We stress this not only because it is a vital aspect of consideration for any teacher research such as the TWS but because it also allows us to focus on the creation of the TWS and its action research components as an ongoing process rather than a product in and of itself. It is easy for many teacher candidates to begin viewing the TWS as a product—something to be completed, a requirement to be fulfilled, an assignment to be graded for a course or, even more important, to be eligible for a teaching license.

At its core, TWS is not about a product but rather a process; the process of developing teachers who are able to systematically examine and document evidence from their own teaching that supports student learning. How are teachers encouraged to develop this ability? Not merely through creating the goals and objectives, lessons, and assessments that compose a TWS. Certainly not merely through the creation of charts and graphs that display student outcomes, but definitely through the critical, continued, and deep reflection upon teaching that occurs throughout the TWS both on a daily and holistic basis.

TWS methodology aims to create teachers who are reflective practitioners who examine their own teaching and reflect upon how it impacts students in their classroom. It is then about developing a habit of mind or reflection-in-action mindset that encourages continual, critical, and systematic examination of one's own teaching practices and outcomes.

The emphasis on creating a reflective teaching mindset and set of professional skills and habits strongly ties TWS methodology to the aims of action research, to develop professional teachers who are able to critically examine their own practice through the lens of student learning and continually seek to improve upon their practice to benefit students. Critical, systematic reflection on teaching, asking the questions about how well students are learning what we intend to teach, and continually seeking to improve practice to benefit student learning—these are perhaps the strongest hopes we have to improve the lives of both teachers and students in today's schools.

It may sometimes be tempting while within the process of creating the TWS to ask that old student mantra, "When will I ever do this again?" Although we admit that you may not create a formal written TWS after your graduation and licensure as a teacher, we firmly hope that the process involved in both action research and the TWS, the reflection-in-action mindset, will become an integral part of your professional habits and identity as a teacher.

## QUESTIONS FOR REVIEW AND REFLECTION

1. Using the framework of considering "learners, learning outcomes, and teaching strategy," practice constructing two or three research questions that might work for a unit of study or TWS you are about to construct.
2. After you construct two to three questions, identify data sources you can collect that will purposefully address those questions.
3. Who can you call on for professional support as you construct your TWS through the lens of action research—consider resources from both the university and your field placement.
4. How do you envision your TWS promoting student learning and developing your skillfulness as a teacher?
5. How does blending TWSM within the framework of action research strengthen an emphasis on student learning? Why might universities want to consider encouraging an "action in research" mindset with teacher candidates?

## REFERENCES

Cochran-Smith, M. (2008). The new teacher education in the United States: Directions forward. *Teachers and teaching: Theory and practice, 14* (4), 271–82.

Cochran-Smith, M. (2006). Ten promising trends (and three big worries). *Educational Leadership, 63* (6), 20–25.

Coleman, J. S., Campbell, E. Q., Hobson, C. J., McPartland, J., Mood, A. M., Weinfeld, F. D., York, R. L. (1966). Equality of educational opportunity. Washington, DC: U.S. Governmental Printing Office.

Darling-Hammond, L., & Bransford, J. (2005). *Preparing teachers for a changing world.* San Francisco: Jossey-Bass.

Denner, P., Norman, A. D., Salzman, S. A., & Pankratz, R. S. (2003). Connecting teaching performance to student achievement: A generalizability and validity study of the Renaissance Teacher Work Sample Assessment. *Paper presented at the Annual Meeting of the Association of Teacher Educators, Jacksonville, FL.*

Denner, P., Salzman, S. A., & Bangert, A. W. (2001). Linking teacher assessment to student performance: A benchmarking, generalizabilty, and validity study on the use of teacher work samples. *Journal of Personnel Evaluation in Education, 15* (4), 287–307.

Gelberg, D. (2007). The business agenda for school reform: A parallel universe. *Teacher Education Quarterly, 34* (2), 45–58.

Girod, M. (2008). Deepening understanding of the teaching and learning context through ethnographic analysis. *The Teacher Educator, 43* (3), 1–23.

Gore, J., & Zeichner, K. (1991). Action research and reflective teaching in pre-service teacher education: A case study from the United States. *Teaching and Teacher Education, 7*(2), 119–36.

Goswami, D., & Rutherford, R. (2009). "What's going on here?": Seeking answers through teacher inquiry. In Goswami, D., Lewis, C., Rutherford, M., & Waff, D. (Eds.). *Teacher inquiry: Approaches to language and literacy research* (pp. 1–11). New York: Teachers College Press.

Grossman, P. (2008). Responding to our critics: From crisis to opportunity in research on teacher education. *Journal of Teacher Education, 59* (1), 10–23.

Hubbard, R., & Power, B. (2003). *The art of classroom inquiry: A handbook for yeacher-researchers.* Portsmouth, NH: Heinnemann.

Jessop, T. S., & Penney, A. J. (1999). A story behind a story: Developing strategies for making sense of teacher narratives. *International Journal of Social Research Methodology, 2*(3), 213–30.

National Commission on Teaching and America's Future. (1996). *What matters most: Teaching for America's future.* New York: Author.

Nieto, S. (2005). Public schools and the work of teachers. In. S. Nieto (Ed.), *Why we teach* (pp. 3–11). New York: Teachers College Press.

Schalock, H. D., & Myton, D. (1988). A new paradigm for teacher licensure: Oregon's demand for evidence of success in fostering learning. *Journal of Teacher Education, 38* (8), 8–16.

Schalock, H. D., Schalock, M., & Girod, G. (1997). Teacher work sample methodology as used at Western Oregon State College. In J. Millman (Ed.) *Grading teachers, grading schools.* Thousand Oaks, CA: Corwin Press.

Shambaugh, N., & Webb-Dempsey, J. (2008). Focusing the study: Framing a researchable question. In Lassonde, C. A., & Israel, S. (Eds.). *Teachers taking action: A comprehensive guide to teacher research* (pp. 29–43). Newark, DE: International Reading Association.

Shepard, L. (2001). The role of classroom assessment in teaching and learning. In Richardson, V. (Ed.). *Handbook of research on teaching,* 4th ed. (pp. 1066–101). New York: American Educational Research Association.

Valli, L. (2000). Connecting teacher development and school improvement: Ironic consequences of a pre-service action research course. *Teaching and Teacher Education, 16*(7), 715–30.

# 7

# Action Research to Change Student Behavior

*Debi Gartland, PhD, Professor, Department of Special Education, Towson University, Maryland*

## INTRODUCTION

You have no doubt heard teachers lament that they could get much more instruction in if they weren't spending as much time in disciplining. Maybe you have expressed frustration at puzzling or challenging student behavior in your field placements. It is likely that you had several "methods" courses during your initial stage of preparation, focusing on *what* and *how* to teach. However, many teacher preparation programs do not require even a basic classroom management course. Those that do often do not include information about students with more severe behavior needs.

If you had a classroom management course, you may find the tools you were taught will be sufficient most of the time, but for some of your students who exhibit difficult behavior, you will need a more in-depth analysis of their behavior. That's when your action research skills will come in handy. And, as you will experience if you are lucky enough to have a long happy career in education, classroom management is best learned on the job and your style will be ever evolving. If your classroom management course did not discuss behavior using the action research process, this chapter is for you.

## CHAPTER OBJECTIVES

By the time you finish reading and thinking about this chapter you will be able to:

- Articulate how action research is used to improve student behavior.
- Describe Functional Behavioral Assessment.
- List the essential components of a Behavioral Intervention Plan.
- Identify developmentally-appropriate supports to use with your students.

## ACTION RESEARCH AND BEHAVIORAL OUTCOMES

As earlier chapters in this book indicated, you know that action research is ideal for increasing your students' academic outcomes. In this chapter, you will learn how to apply the action research process to your students' behaviors. Action research may be used to improve a teaching strategy to yield higher student achievement or you may engage in the process to tackle a problem. This chapter will deal with the latter, namely how to improve your students' behaviors, which in turn will yield more positive student academic outcomes. In contrast to more traditional, punitive classroom management, there is a well established research base of positive strategies to quell the majority of behavior problems that will arise in your internships. Thus, action research has emerged as a process to be used with all students to achieve long-term, positive behavior.

Many initial certification or licensure teacher preparation programs assign an action research project as a requirement of the major or for graduation. Often special education teacher candidates must complete an action research project designed to change a student's inappropriate behavior. When inappropriate behavior begins to interfere with a student's academic achievement or social standing, something needs to occur to curtail, reduce the impact of, or eliminate the undesired behaviors.

This chapter will assist you, the teacher candidate, to affect change in students' behaviors. It will guide you in how to design an action research plan using the five-step process described in chapter 1. You will be able to successfully identify the behavior issue interfering with your student's success. You will then learn how to collect data using Functional Behavioral Assessment and, subsequently, develop, implement, and evaluate an action plan, called a Behavior Intervention Plan. Using the action research process, you will learn when you will need to cycle back to earlier steps if you are not yet satisfied with student's resultant behavior.

## APPLYING THE FIVE STEP ACTION RESEARCH PROCESS TO BEHAVIORAL GOALS

As discussed in chapter 1, many teachers use the action research process to improve their students' academic achievements. You can apply the same Five Step Action Research process to improve your students' behaviors. The process is generally the same, requiring you to be reflective in your practice and cycle back to earlier steps if you are not satisfied with the results yielded. What follows is an elaboration of each of the following five steps applied to your students' behaviors:

1. Issue Identification
2. Data Collection
3. Action Planning
4. Plan Activation
5. Outcome Assessment

### Step 1: Issue Identification

The first step in the action research process is issue identification. Think about the last classroom you were in. What were the typical inappropriate behaviors you encountered? In any elementary, middle, or high school, you might see students whose inappropriate behaviors range in their impact on learning from those who constantly call out, incessantly talk with neighboring students, or are unable to stay on task to those students who are noncompliant, aggressive, or even prone to violent outbursts. Did you notice a difference in how often the inappropriate behaviors occur based on the *activity* (i.e., math class, reading groups, science labs) or the *setting* (i.e., transitioning to art, in the cafeteria, on a fieldtrip) or the *task demand* (i.e., during seatwork, getting to class on time, giving an oral presentation)? Depending upon the nature of and how often these behaviors were exhibited, the classroom teacher might have consequated them differently.

All teacher candidates will encounter students with challenging behaviors sometime in their teacher preparation field experiences. The severity of the impact of those behaviors will vary. What cannot vary is whether to intervene; although how, how often, and when to intervene will vary. Addressing student behavior is part of a teacher's responsibility.

Although ultimately it is up to the student to decide how to act, the teacher must be confident that he did everything to ensure that the student had full knowledge of the rules, procedures, expectations, and consequences. Students must be taught to take full responsibility of their actions.

Teachers cannot allow students to blame others or their circumstances for their behavior. No doubt, you may encounter students whose life situations are sad. Regardless, it would be a disservice to allow students to go on acting inappropriately, without feedback from you.

You should intervene when: (1) the student's behavior is interfering with your ability to teach effectively or the student's own learning or that of others; (2) the student's grades or other achievement indicators are on the decline; (3) other students start to complain about the student's behavior or socially isolate the student; (4) there is an increase in office referrals or points lost in a class or schoolwide system; (5) the student has been identified as having a disability and has an Individualized Education Program (IEP) (see the next section for further discussion); and (6) your teacher voice (which does get stronger the more you teach!) tells you something isn't quite right with the student.

### A Few Words about the Individuals with Disabilities Improvement Act of 2004

As noted, all teacher candidates will encounter students in their internships who exhibit challenging behavior, regardless of whether these students are typically developing or students with disabilities on Individualized Education Programs (IEPs). It's important to note, too, that not all students with disabilities have challenging behaviors. Regardless if you are majoring or minoring in special education or in general education, all interns will need to know how to address student behavior.

As you probably learned in an introductory special education course, the federal special education law states that positive behavioral interventions and supports must be considered in the case of a student with a disability whose behavior impedes the student's learning or that of other students.

The student with a disability must receive a Functional Behavioral Assessment (FBA) and a Behavioral Intervention Plan (BIP) and modifications designed to address the student's behavior if the IEP team determines that the behavior is a "manifestation" of the disability—that is, if the behavior has a direct and substantial relationship to the student's disability. FBAs and BIPs must also be used proactively, however, if the IEP team determines that they would be appropriate for the student. If the student already has a BIP and continues to behave inappropriately, the IEP team will need to review the plan and modify it, as necessary, to address the behavior.

You should also know that parental consent is required to conduct a FBA if the student has an IEP. A FBA is an individualized evaluation of a student to assist in determining whether the student is, or continues to be, a student with a disability. As such, the FBA process is frequently used to determine the nature and extent of the special education and related services that the student needs, including the need for a BIP. Behavior goals, then, may become part of the student's IEP. Again, although a FBA and BIP must be used when a student with a disability is exhibiting behavior problems, they are successfully used with students who do not have IEPs.

## Step 2: Data Collection

The second step in the action research process is data collection. Data are essential in any action research project you undertake. After you have identified your student's behavior as an issue, and your aim is to change your

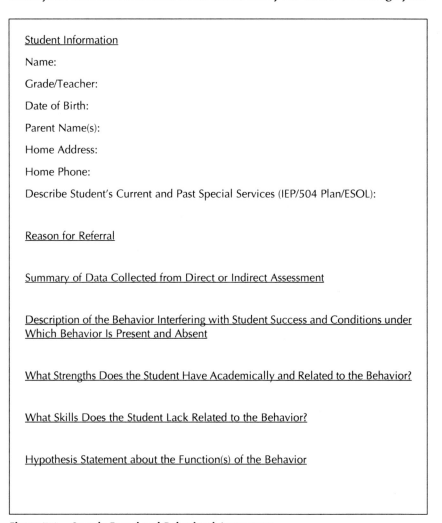

Student Information

Name:

Grade/Teacher:

Date of Birth:

Parent Name(s):

Home Address:

Home Phone:

Describe Student's Current and Past Special Services (IEP/504 Plan/ESOL):

Reason for Referral

Summary of Data Collected from Direct or Indirect Assessment

Description of the Behavior Interfering with Student Success and Conditions under Which Behavior Is Present and Absent

What Strengths Does the Student Have Academically and Related to the Behavior?

What Skills Does the Student Lack Related to the Behavior?

Hypothesis Statement about the Function(s) of the Behavior

**Figure 7.1. Sample Functional Behavioral Assessment**

student's behavior, you conduct a functional behavioral assessment (FBA), which is often pronounced "f'bah." With the guidance of your mentor teacher, you must develop a plan for conducting a FBA. A well developed FBA will help you identify the contextual factors that contribute to behavior. This information will allow you to predict the circumstances under which the inappropriate behavior is likely to occur. A sample Functional Behavioral Assessment is provided in Figure 7.1.

A FBA is a systematic process, incorporating an array of strategies and techniques. It is used to pinpoint the problem behavior, describe the settings under which behavior is and is not likely to occur, and identify the function (the why) of the problem behavior. A FBA is an integral component in designing an effective behavior support plan. The information yielded is used to identify and teach more appropriate replacement behaviors and to develop an effective plan to eliminate or reduce the occurrence or severity of the problem behavior.

Although there are numerous ways to conduct a FBA, the general pattern is to collect information about your student's problem behavior, propose a testable explanation, and then assess the validity of your hypothesis. To begin, you and your mentor need to make several key decisions based on answers to the following questions:

- Do you need to secure parental permission to collect data?
- Who will collect the data?
- Which behavior will you target first?
- Is there an existing assessment sensitive to measure the targeted behavior?

*Parental Permission*

Because of the additional protections of federal and state special education laws, it is often best to gain permission from the parents of your students with disabilities who have Individualized Education Programs (IEPs). Also consider whether special circumstances, such as students who have 504 plans or who are English Language Learners, might warrant your obtaining permission. Additionally, your mentor might alert you to parents who expect you to keep them in the loop more so than other parents because they may be sensitive to having their child singled out. If you are unsure, and because you are focusing in on behavior rather than pure academics, it is better to err on the safe side and ask the parent for permission. However, in most cases, parental permission is not needed at this juncture because the action research process is really just part of good teaching.

*Collecting the Data*

This is especially important to consider if you want to collect data across different settings (i.e., different teachers, recess, locker rooms). If two adults are in the room, data collection is easier for the one staff member who is not primarily responsible for instruction that class period so that adult can concentrate solely on the targeted student. You need to collect the data unobtrusively—that is collecting the data so the student is unaware so the behavior is not affected, thus tainting the data and your subsequent analysis. If someone other than you will be collecting the data, you will need to ensure that each person is collecting the data on the same behavior and in the same manner or else you will not get a clear picture of what is really going on.

*Targeting the Behavior*

When you collect data, you need to hone in on a specific behavior and avoid making the rookie mistake of trying to collect data on too many things at once. You might need to prioritize which behaviors are interfering more than others, or better yet, what is the behavior keeping a child, or other children, from meeting with success in your classroom. We like to call this the "most intrusive" behavior. That should become your "target behavior" for change.

*Assessing the Behavior*

Is there a tool your mentor has used with success to collect data on student behaviors? Is there someone else in the school that might have a useful tool? You could check with other teachers, the guidance counselor or school psychologist as well as other interns and your college professors for various approaches to track and begin to identify specific problematic behaviors. Simple tools can include a record of time outs and why they occurred, office referrals (which includes the reason for the referral), or perhaps you keep a daily reflection journal of what is occurring in your classroom.

The point is to keep it simple. You do not need to re-create a tool when you can borrow or adapt an existing tool. Remember, good teachers know when to recognize others' great ideas and adapt them to fit their own circumstances. If an appropriate tool does not exist, you might find it productive to enlist others to assist you in developing an appropriate tool that will be sensitive enough (usually providing some specific details) to provide you with useful data.

*Understanding "Functions" of Behaviors*

There is general agreement in the field of education that there is no single cause for problem behaviors. The causes or "functions" of students' behaviors can be very different. If you only attend to the overt topography (what the behavior looks like in your internship classroom), you will get little information about the appropriate intervention. If however, you work to identify the underlying cause(s) (what the student "gets" or "avoids" through the inappropriate behavior), you and others collaborating with you on the student's behavior will be able to develop proactive strategies (i.e., the positive behavioral interventions and supports) to help guide the student to make better behavior decisions.

You must first identify the intent or functions the inappropriate behaviors serve before you can then teach your student alternative, school- and socially-appropriate behavior which satisfy the same function as the inappropriate behavior. The inappropriate behavior is often a result of several factors, including the student's past history, observation of others, and limited repertoire of alternative, more appropriate behaviors. Remember, too, the function of the student's behavior is not typically considered inappropriate. Rather, the resultant behavior itself is judged to be appropriate or not.

Problem behaviors serve a function for the student. Even though the challenging behaviors may be socially inappropriate, they are driven by the belief that they will produce a desired result for the student. Typical functions of students' inappropriate behaviors are: (1) avoiding or escaping a task or demand; (2) obtaining attention of teachers or peers; (3) gaining control over the situation or others; (4) obtaining a desired object or activity; and, (5) satisfying sensory needs.

To set the stage for meaningful long-term behavior change in your student, you must answer the following questions: What is the function of my student's behavior? Does the same inappropriate behavior serve different functions? Do different behaviors serve the same function for my student? For example, Lee dislikes science labs so Lee constantly cracks jokes, which makes class members laugh, disrupting instruction. The teacher is fed up with Lee's behavior and this time sends Lee to the office. What function does this serve for Lee? Lee both gains attention and avoids a low-interest subject. The following are examples of inappropriate behaviors and the possible functions:

- Calling out—*seeking peer attention*
- Out of seat—*avoiding academic task*
- Lying about homework completion—*escaping undesirable work*
- Delaying the start of seatwork—*avoiding math classwork*

- Asking off-task questions—*both seeking teacher attention and avoiding work*
- Defiance in completing work—*escaping embarrassment of showing academic weakness*

*Assessment Measures*

There are many different ways to collect data on your student's behavior. Your goal is to define the behavior in concrete terms that are simple to communicate and easy to measure and record. Some examples of how to "frame" language so it is simple and measurable might include:

| *Instead of saying:* | *Say:* |
|---|---|
| Lee was aggressive. | Lee kicked Pat in the lunch line. |
| Riley is disruptive. | Riley makes irrelevant remarks during reading group. |
| Delaney is hyperactive. | Delaney leaves her seat without adult permission. |

Because the problem behavior may serve several functions for your student, you need to use a multitude of sources, collecting data both directly and indirectly.

*Direct Assessment Measures*

Direct assessment measures require you to observe and record the situational factors or context surrounding the inappropriate behavior. *A-B-C, matrix,* and *scatter plot charts* are examples of direct assessment measures.

**A-B-C Charts** When you collect data using an A-B-C chart, you will need to collect data across different settings, activities, and school subjects. You will examine this data in light of (A) Antecedents, (B) Behaviors, and (C) Consequences. A sample *A-B-C Chart* is provided for you in figure 7.2.

*A-Antecedents:* The antecedent describes what happens before the behavior. In other words, what was the student doing just before the behavior was exhibited or emitted? How long had the student been engaging in that activity? Who else was present and what were they doing? Did they say anything to the student that might have set the student "off" or affected the student's behavior? You are trying to figure out what events occurred just prior to the behavior that might have acted as a trigger for the behavior.

*B-Behaviors:* You need to describe the behavior in observable and measurable terms such that anyone not present when the student exhibited the behavior would have the same understanding of what went on just by your description. What exactly did the student do? To answer that, you need to

| Student: _____ | Observer: _____ |
|---|---|
| Setting of Observation: _____ | Start/End Time: _____ |
| Class Period/Subject: _____ | Class Activity: _____ |

| Date | Antecedent | Behavior | Consequence |
|---|---|---|---|
|  |  |  |  |
|  |  |  |  |
|  |  |  |  |
|  |  |  |  |

**Figure 7.2.   A-B-C Chart**

operationally define the behavior. Behavior might be described by various parameters, including *frequency, duration, latency,* and *magnitude.* Not all behaviors can be easily described using all four parameters. Remember your goal is to paint a picture for the people who were not present, so select the best parameter(s) to describe what happened.

1. *Frequency*—Frequency is how often a behavior occurred in a certain period of time. Behaviors that are easily described using frequency would be calling out or swearing.
2. *Duration*—Duration is how long the behavior lasted. Behaviors that are easily described using duration would be crying or having a tantrum.
3. *Latency*—Latency is the time that elapsed between when you asked the student to do something and when the student started to comply with your request. Behaviors that are easily described using latency would be the amount of time that passes after you call your math group to the small table and when your student arrives or how long it takes a child to stop tapping the pencil on the desk after you told the child to stop.
4. *Magnitude*—Magnitude is the force with which the behavior occurred. Behaviors that are easily described using magnitude would be hitting or kicking.

Behaviors are context related in that they are in response to the student's environment what is going on in the student's immediate situation will dictate how the student chooses to act. The behavior the student selects may be consciously or unconsciously made.

*C-Consequences:* The consequence describes what happened after the behavior occurred. How did other students and school personnel respond to the student? What was said to the student? How was the behavior stopped? Did the student stop on his own, or did others intervene to stop the student? What did the student do after the behavior was stopped?

**Matrix and Scatter Plot Charts**   *Matrix* (figure 7.3) and *Scatter Plot Charts* (figure 7.4) show the relationship between the student's behavior and instructional task demands. They help you visually display when and how often the inappropriate behavior is occurring. You can design these tools to be tailor made to fit you and your student's circumstances.

### Indirect Assessment Measures

You need to figure out what the payoff is for the student engaging in inappropriate behavior. In other words, what does the student escape, avoid,

---

Student: _____   Observer: _____

Setting of Observation: _____   Start/End Time: _____

Class Period/Subject: _____

Class Activity & Expectations for Behavior: _____
_____
_____

| *insert your class tasks across here* → | Large Group Activity | Small Group Activity | Independent Work | Silent Reading | Math Game | Book Quiz |
|---|---|---|---|---|---|---|
| *Insert the targeted behaviors below:* | | | | | | |
| Off-task | | | | | | |
| Calling Out | | | | | | |
| Out-of-seat | | | | | | |

*personalize your coding and rate of occurrence below:*

Code for marking matrix:
  X = persistent behavior (occurring 50% or more of the time)
  / = present but low rate of behavior (occurring 50% or less)

**Figure 7.3.   Matrix**

Student: _____ Observer: _____

Setting of Observation: _____ Start/End Time: _____

Class Period/Subject: _____

Class Activity & Expectations for Behavior: _____
_____
_____

*personalize dates and timeframe:*

|  | 10/1 | 10/2 | 10/3 | 10/4 | 10/5 |
|---|---|---|---|---|---|
| 10:00-10:15 |  |  |  |  |  |
| 10:30-10:45 |  |  |  |  |  |
| 10:45-11:00 |  |  |  |  |  |
| 11:00-11:15 |  |  |  |  |  |

*personalize your coding below:*

Code for marking scatter plot:
   no mark  =  on task
   X  =  off task

**Figure 7.4. Scatter Plot**

or get? To fully understand the contextual factors, you need to supplement information you gather from direct measures with *indirect assessment measures* to uncover unobserved cognitive and affective behaviors. For example, if your student acts out each time you assign math seatwork, it may indicate that the problem behavior is linked to a *skill deficit*. Your student may lack the skills to perform the expected task so the student acts out in order to escape or avoid the math seatwork. On the other hand, if you know your student has the prerequisite skills necessary to perform the task but chooses not to use the skill consistently, this is referred to as a *performance deficit*. The consequences, such as non-performance attention from the teacher, may be reinforcing so the student does not perform the task.

Indirect assessment measures include structured interviews with the student, teachers and other school personnel as well as the student's parents. Questionnaires, motivational scales, and checklists can also be useful indirect measures. You will want to confer with your mentor, guidance counselor, and school psychologist for the best measures for your student. You will also want to do a record review to ascertain if this or similar behavior issues have been noted about your student by previous teachers and to see any other noteworthy information that might be pertinent to your student's current behavior. Look for factors such as attendance records, health history, family issues, discipline referrals, results from previous education or behavior assessments and accompanying interventions.

Remember, regardless of which tools you use, you need to observe across time and situations and gather both quantitative and qualitative information. If you are not able to discern patterns from your data, you need to gather additional data. Drawing from an analysis of your data, you need to establish a hypothesis (i.e., a plausible explanation) for the function served by your student's behavior. Once the FBA is completed, you and others involved meet to develop an intervention plan, which is discussed in the next section of this chapter.

### Step 3: Action Planning

The third step in the action research process is action planning. Once you are satisfied that you have collected enough data, you will want to analyze what you have. This will assist you in clarifying your student's behavior patterns.

Drawing from your analysis and discerned patterns, you are ready to put forth a hypothesis regarding the function(s) of the inappropriate behavior, which in turn will enable you to develop a plan crafted to address problem behaviors that interfere with your student's social and academic success. This plan is called an individual Behavioral Intervention Plan (BIP), which is often pronounced "bip." You might have heard related terms such as Positive Behavior Support Plan (PBSP) or Positive Behavioral Interventions and Supports (PBIS), which refer to the same type of intervention plan but whose names emphasize the positive (rather than punitive) nature of the plans and necessary supports that must be put in place to address behaviors which impede learning and assist the student to make good behavior decisions. Regardless of what you have heard, you should find out the preferred term in your internship school and use that consistently.

PBIS is a research-based approach looking at behavior in the context of the setting in which the behavior occurs. You or a network of adults in the student's life designs environments to support improved, more appropriate behavior. Whereas traditional approaches focus on changing the student, the focus of the BIP is on changing the environment in which the student learns. The goal of a BIP is to eliminate inappropriate behaviors and replace them with more appropriate behaviors. The approach is used with individual students or entire school populations. It is important to note that even with an effective schoolwide plan and sufficient supports in place, some of your students will require a BIP tailored to their needs, so you should not assume your classroom management skills are at fault. Remember, too, the more closely aligned the BIP is with the results of the FBA, the more success you are likely to experience.

After you have collected data and identified the function, you need to develop a BIP. The plan should include positive strategies, any necessary curricular modifications, and supplementary aids and supports necessary to address both the problem behavior and the source of the problem. As appropriate to your student's circumstances, the BIP should include plans to:

- Increase the rates of existing appropriate behaviors.
- Teach socially appropriate replacement behaviors that serve the same functions as the inappropriate behaviors.
- Make changes in the student's environment so as to discourage the student from acting inappropriately.
- Provide supports necessary to elicit the more appropriate replacement behaviors.

### Increasing the Rates of Existing Appropriate Behaviors

You need to ensure that the student knows what the behavioral expectations are and, if not, your plan would outline how this will be accomplished. It would then include the plan to teach expectations and the supports, aids, and strategies to accomplish the goal. It is important to remember not to coerce your student into being compliant as that will only improve behavior in the short term and may, in fact, lead to more drastic problem behaviors. Of course, in designing any classroom management plan, a goal should always be to treat students with dignity and respect. Remember, too, to provide plenty of opportunities for the student to earn positive reinforcement for appropriate behaviors and remove any rewards that may inadvertently reinforcing misbehaviors.

### Teaching Socially Appropriate Replacement Behaviors that Serve the Same Functions as the Inappropriate Behaviors

As you know, reactive discipline procedures will only address the symptoms of the problem so the problem behavior is likely to occur again until the underlying causes are addressed. Once you have clearly defined the inappropriate behavior as well as the function it serves for your student, you are ready to select a more prosocial behavior that would allow the student to obtain the same desired result. You then develop a workable plan that teaches and supports the replacement behavior.

*Making Changes in the Student's Environment so as to Discourage the Student from Acting Inappropriately*

Your hypothesis as to why the student acts inappropriately under certain conditions will lead to specific intervention strategies. The plan should eliminate or at least decrease opportunities for your student to engage in the inappropriate behavior. This means that you need to eliminate or alter antecedents and setting factors that trigger the misbehavior. You should also identify and provide additional antecedents which will facilitate the occurrence of appropriate behavior. Your aim is to give your student more frequent access to what your student desires so that the undesired behavior is no longer necessary. To do this, you must manipulate various conditions that exist in your student's environment which cause your student to repeat the inappropriate behavior. The BIP must ensure that the antecedents and sometimes the consequences are manipulated.

The plan may call for adjustments in instructional strategies or curricula. If the problem behavior results from a *skill deficit* in which the student does not know how to perform certain skills, you outline how and when you will teach or remediate the specific academic skills your student lacks.

Also consider that your student may not know that he is engaging in inappropriate behavior. The inappropriate behavior may now be occurring out of habit or lack of social awareness or be associated with a disability. If so, your plan would need to teach your student to recognize when he is engaging in the inappropriate behavior as well as provide training, for example, in social skills, problem-solving techniques, or anger management, based on what your student is lacking in the social realm.

If the problem behavior results from a *performance deficit* in which the student knows how to perform certain skills but does not consistently perform them, the BIP should include strategies and supports designed to motivate the student to perform the skill. In addition to skill and motivation factors, and depending upon what the FBA revealed, the BIP may need to include changes to the learning environment. Antecedents to the problem behavior may indicate that the proximity of your student's desk to a neighbor's warrants a change in the physical arrangement of furniture in your class. Additionally, academic tasks that are too easy or boring might be precursors to problem behavior and need to be adjusted.

*Provide Supports Necessary to Elicit the More Appropriate Replacement Behaviors*

After you have taught your student a replacement behavior that serves the same function as the inappropriate behavior, you must now factor in scaffolds to encourage the use of the appropriate behavior. Ask yourself, what should be built into your student's learning environment to support your student to make good behavior decisions?

If you don't already know your student well, you might want develop a reinforcement menu such as the one in figure 7.5. The student can then rate or select what reinforcers the student wants as a reward or support. Your reinforcement menu should be tailored to be developmentally appropriate.

An effective support for a younger student, such as eating lunch with the teacher, may, in fact, be construed a punishment for an older student! Remember, too, to monitor the potency of the reward: If the student's behavior does not improve, then the reinforcer is not as potent as you want it to be and you should guide the student to select a more potent reinforcer. Initially, you might find better success with extrinsic motivators while encouraging your student to behave for intrinsic motivators. For example, you might consider putting in place a behavioral contract or token economy to support your student's behavior. You will want input from your mentor on a plan to fade out extrinsic reinforcers by gradually replacing them with intrinsic rewards, possibly by pairing them as you start to the fading out process.

Remember that school personnel may serve as a source of supports. Counselors and school psychologists are trained to work with groups as well as with individuals. Don't overlook how peers, front office, and custodial staff might also serve as supports.

Finally, it is important to build into the process an evaluation plan. You want to ensure you monitor the fidelity with which the Behavior In-

---

Examples of Supports

Sticker charts

Positive phone calls home

Computer time

Token economy

Homework pass

Teacher-for-a-Day

Extra Art time

"If-Then" visual prompts

Activity choice

Behavioral contract

---

**Figure 7.5.   Reinforcement Menu**

tervention Plan (BIP) is being implemented. In other words, you want to make sure everyone involved is consistently carrying out the plan as it was intended. A second part of your evaluation plan is how you will measure the plan's success. Has your student's behavior improved, consistent with the goals of the BIP? If not, it's back to the FBA-drawing board to collect more data or make adjustments to the plan. An example BIP is provided in figure 7.6.

### Step 4: Plan Activation

You have formulated a hypothesis based on the data, explaining the relationship between the behavior, antecedents, consequences, and func-

Student Information

Name:

Grade/Teacher:

Date of Birth:

Parent Name(s):

Home Address:

Home Phone:

Describe Student's Current and Past Special Services (IEP/504 Plan/ESOL):

Summary of Inappropriate Behavior(s), Function(s) Served, Conditions Under Which Behavior(s) are Present and Absent, and Replacement Behavior(s)

Strategies to Prevent the Inappropriate Behavior(s)

Strategies to Teach Replacement Behavior(s)

Curricular Modifications, Supplementary Aids and Supports Needed to Maintain Replacement Behavior(s)

Implementation, Documentation, Evaluation, and Review Plans

**Figure 7.6. Sample Behavior Intervention Plan**

tion served by the behavior. You have developed an action plan and are now ready to put the BIP into place. You must validate your hypothesis by establishing the conditions under which the inappropriate behavior does and does not occur and then demonstrating the behavior in the presence of conditions that trigger that behavior. If you cannot validate your hypothesis with the conditions you identified (i.e., the student does not exhibit the inappropriate behavior), you need to cycle back through the action research process to data collection and a reformulation of your hypothesis.

Once you are satisfied that your BIP is appropriate, it is finally time to activate it. As implementation occurs, you must formatively assess the progress your student is making behaviorally and, again, make adjustments to your plan accordingly.

## Step 5: Outcome Assessment

You become a better teacher each time you conduct an action research project, as you are adding to your knowledge and skills about the teaching-learning relationship. Each subsequent student with challenging behaviors who you encounter will benefit from the thoughtful process in which you engaged as part of your action research.

As discussed in chapter 1, now is the time to share your results. How will you report on progress to others? Typical ways to share your news may include through seminar presentation to fellow interns and college faculty members. At school, your mentor teacher may ask you to share your findings at a parent-teacher conference or at an IEP meeting if the student has a disability. School administrators may also be interested in your behavior change data as a way to inform the school improvement plan. Celebrate what you learned, how your student's behavior has improved, and reflect on how to incorporate your new knowledge into your class management.

## QUESTIONS FOR REVIEW AND REFLECTION

1. How can you use the action research process to change student behavior?
2. How can you "track" behaviors?
3. Why is it important to identify the function a behavior serves for a student?
4. What is a functional behavioral assessment?
5. What is a behavior intervention plan?
6. Why should you describe behaviors in measurable terms?

# 8

# Response to Intervention: A Framework for Action Research

*David Hoppey, PhD, Associate Professor, Department of Special Education, West Virginia University*

*Aimee Morewood, PhD, Assistant Professor, Department of Curriculum and Instruction, Literacy Studies, West Virginia University*

*Johnna Bolyard, PhD, Assistant Professor, Department of Curriculum and Instruction, Literacy Studies, West Virginia University*

## INTRODUCTION

The No Child Left Behind Act (NCLB 2002) charges schools with the responsibility of ensuring that "all children have a fair, equal, and significant opportunity to obtain a high-quality education." This means that schools and teachers must make every effort to meet the needs of all students, including those who are not achieving at an acceptable level of proficiency, regardless of reason.

In this spirit, the Individuals with Disabilities Education Act (IDEA), reauthorized in 2004, shifted focus away from identification of students with learning disabilities based on discrepancies between their IQ scores and their academic achievement toward examining students' response to research-based instruction and intervention (Fuchs & Fuchs 2007; Fuchs, Fuchs, Compton, Bouton, Caffey, & Hill 2007; Stecker, Fuchs, & Fuchs 2008). This approach, known as *Response to Intervention* (*RtI*) focuses on early intervention efforts to identify and address the needs of all students who are not achieving at desired levels.

The RtI approach is different from a discrepancy approach in its focus on students' responses to high quality, research-based instruction and interventions (Fuchs, Compton, Fuchs, Paulsen, Bryant, & Hamlett 2007; Ysseldyke, Burns, Scholin, & Parker 2010).

As states and districts begin to require that schools implement RtI, teachers must understand and know how to weave the process into their instruction. The RtI system requires teachers to examine how their students learn through the process of employing research-based instructional approaches, continually collecting data for the purposes of monitoring students' responses to instruction, and making instructional decisions based on these data. These steps all occur within the context of the specific school and classroom and with respect to each individual child's background and unique needs. The cycle shifts through multiple tiers, distinguished by different levels of targeted intervention.

RtI provides teachers with opportunities to closely examine, reflect upon, and learn about their own practice and their students' learning. It is a natural fit with action research. In this chapter, we will describe how the RtI process provides a framework for you to engage in action research that will enable you to determine how your students respond to instruction. Further, this chapter will provide you with opportunity to reflect upon this knowledge so that you can design a plan for better meeting the needs of all students.

## CHAPTER OBJECTIVES

By the time you finish reading and thinking about this chapter you will be able to:

- Define RtI
- Describe the implications of RtI on teacher preparation
- Describe RtI as a framework for action research
- Describe how engaging in RtI as action research aligns with the *reflection-in-action* mindset
- Align the elements of RtI with the five stages of the action research process
- Describe why action research on the RtI model is important
- Describe action research projects on the RtI model

## RESPONSE TO INTERVENTION OVERVIEW

Response to Intervention (RtI) is a multi-tiered intervention model currently in various stages of implementation across the nation. RtI as outlined in federal legislation (NCLB 2002; IDEA 2004) highlights the importance of providing high quality instruction that not only is tied to achieving high academic standards but also is differentiated to meet the individual needs of all students. Essential to the success of implementing the RtI process are five components that all preservice and in-service teachers need to have knowledge of:

- Tiered instructional models;
- Scientifically research-based instruction;
- Ongoing assessment including universal screening and progress monitoring;
- Teaming and collaboration; and
- Data-based decision making (Fuchs & Fuchs 2006; 2007; Palenchar & Boyer 2008).

## RTI TIERS OF INSTRUCTION

Most RtI models across the nation currently employ three "tiers" of instruction. Each tier represents a level of services provided to children. Additional services are provided at each successful tier to further meet a child's needs.

### Tier I

Tier I occurs in the general education setting with all students receiving core instruction using a common instructional program that is research based (Kovaleski & Glew 2006). Effective lessons should include a range of scientifically research-based activities, including whole group instruction, small group skill-focused lessons that provide explicit, direct instruction, and work stations to provide multiple practice opportunities and promote high levels of student engagement. Thus, during core instruction, students are exposed to differentiated research-based instruction that is tailored to the different learning needs of students in any given classroom (Deshler, Mellard, Tollefson, & Byrd 2005; Fuchs & Fuchs 2006).

In addition, ongoing assessment is linked to instruction to monitor student achievement. For example, universal screening is one key element of core instruction and includes benchmark screening, diagnostic assessments, and curriculum-based measures (Deno, Reschly, Lembke, Magnusson, Callender, Windram, Stachel 2009). Thus, the purpose of universal screening is twofold: to formally assess students several times each year to measure student progress at chosen intervals at various times throughout the school year and subsequently to identify students who are at-risk and in need of intervention services (Deno et al. 2009; Fuchs & Fuchs 2006).

## Tier II

Tier II interventions take place when students demonstrate deficits in key skills areas on universal screening instruments and curriculum-based classroom data within the core reading or math program. These students participate in small-group supplemental instruction targeting specific skills in their areas of need. These lessons are designed to be student centered and monitor progress regularly. Progress monitoring is frequent, ongoing assessment of targeted skills using curriculum-based measurements to determine the effectiveness of supplemental intervention (Deno et al. 2009, Fuchs & Fuchs 2006).

Consequently, determining student progress requires "data-based decision making derived from observable and measurable outcomes" (Hale, Kauffman, Naglieri, & Kavale 2006, p. 754). This occurs as teachers use results from universal screening and progress-monitoring assessments to determine the effectiveness of instruction at each tier of the RtI model (Roehrig, Guidry, Bodur, Guan, Guo, & Pop 2008; Stecker, Fuchs, & Fuchs 2008). All told, this critical analysis of formative data has the potential to inform the profession on how various instructional and intervention strategies have or have not worked for students (Holdnack & Weiss 2006).

## Tier III

Only small numbers of students should be in need of Tier III interventions. Tier III instruction occurs when the student continues to display deficits in academic performance, despite core instruction and additional learning opportunities in Tier II. Tier III instruction is inherently more individualized, intensive, and prescriptive in nature to address student failure to respond to intervention. In addition, referral and identification for special-education services may occur as students enter this tier but only if all other intervention services have been deemed to be unsuccessful (Bradley, Danielson, & Doolittle 2007; Reschley 2005).

As RtI models continue to be employed across the nation, roles and responsibilities of teachers are likely to change. This shift requires interdisciplinary teams to collaborate effectively by engaging in honest and open communication and sharing knowledge to meet the needs of students who struggle (Hawkins, Kroeger, Musti-Rao, Barnett, & Ward 2008; Moore & Whitfield 2009). For example, as students move between tiers of instruction educators must collaborate on making sound instructional decisions to meet the increasingly diverse needs of our students (Murawski & Hughes 2009). However, these roles are in contrast to the traditional teacher roles assumed in general.

In the past, general educators' primary responsibilities focused on providing core content instruction while their special-education peers were charged with providing strategies and interventions for students who struggle or have disabilities (Mastropieri & Scruggs 2005; Smith & Leonard 2005). The RtI model creates a space where all educators are able to step out of their traditional roles and collaborate to better meet the needs of our students.

## RTI AND STUDENT DATA

As we began to outline the complexities of RtI above, we must also consider teachers' perceptions of how prepared they are to use data efficiently, particularly for students who struggle. For instance, research suggests that while many teachers are skilled at gathering data regarding student achievement, many teachers grapple with how to interpret data to inform their instruction (Mokhtari, Rosemary, & Edwards 2007). In addition, research is emerging that indicates that a teachers' ability to make instructional decisions is dependent upon their professional knowledge and skill of using data (Jacobs, Gregory, Hoppey, & Yendol-Hoppey 2009) and requires analysis of student work that includes informal assessments and student work samples (Jacobs et al. 2009; Mokhtari et al. 2007). Since RtI is a data-driven instructional model, teachers must perceive themselves as *data users* as opposed to *data collectors*.

This change in teacher perspective further complicates teacher education and professional development opportunities as schools, districts, and teacher preparation institutions by creating expectations that preservice and in-service teachers must become data literate, knowledgeable about research-based instructional practices, and understand how to use data-based decisions to guide instruction.

## IMPLICATIONS OF RTI FOR TEACHER PREPARATION

It is critical for you to be responsive to changing trends and be provided opportunities to explore not only research-based best practices but also the dynamics necessary to effectively implement the RtI framework. Therefore, you must understand the proper process of RtI implementation, including the key components stated above and the following challenges.

Research suggests that preservice teachers' preparedness to teach has been drawn into question because they could not demonstrate the basic knowledge needed to teach struggling readers (Bos, Mather, Dickson, Podhajski, & Chard 2001). In addition, research indicates that many preservice teachers were often not able to identify effective instruction in classrooms of their mentor teachers (Roehrig, Duggar, Moats, Glover, & Mincey 2008).

Action research conducted within the RtI model will help you to identify and demonstrate your understanding of effective pedagogical knowledge needed to target all learners.

## RTI AND CLASSROOM INQUIRY

First and foremost, RtI highlights the need for preservice teachers to develop inquiry questions that lend themselves to the action research process. In order to effectively implement strategies and interventions, you must focus these action research topics on scientifically based instruction and data-based decision making. When considering your action research efforts, you should focus on studying the impact research-proven instructional strategies and interventions have on your students' learning.

As you work through your teacher preparation coursework that includes school placements, you will have multiple opportunities to increase your knowledge of and expertise in the core curriculum and intervention strategies. You should view each school placement as a place to gather data on how students learn. Further, you can view different assignments in your coursework as frameworks to guide your action research, such as with RtI. By combining school placements with coursework, you will be able to better understand how action research can help facilitate classroom inquiry, such as with the RtI model.

## ACTION RESEARCH AND RTI

The RtI model creates a space for you to respond to students' individual learning needs. Moreover, the RtI model is data-driven instruction and this is why action research is well suited for the RtI model. The action research process is a vehicle for reflective, responsive teaching. The RtI model offers us many opportunities to engage in the reflective practice and to be responsive teachers, thus moving us toward the reflection-in-action mindset discussed in chapter 1.

Cochran-Smith and Lytle (1999) discuss teacher knowledge as knowledge-for-practice (content knowledge), knowledge-in-practice (practical knowledge), and knowledge-of-practice (knowledge gained through inquiry). This framework helps you to think about how action research can utilize the RtI model to become more responsive to your students' needs. For example, engaging in the RtI model helps you to deepen your content knowledge through various grouping arrangements that target individual student needs.

Further, the RtI model provides opportunities for you to be a reflective practitioner by allowing you to better understand the impact of your instruction on student learning (practical knowledge). Finally, through the RtI model you can begin to question and systematically study your pedagogy to provide more effective instruction (knowledge through inquiry).

Since RtI provides such an excellent frame for action research, you will gain a deeper knowledge of your students (e.g., how they learn concepts and how they develop understandings and/or misconceptions) and a deeper knowledge of the impacts of your pedagogical decisions (e.g., what representations or models or contexts are effective for different students) by implementing this practice.

Action research is clearly aligned with the RtI framework because both are intended to create a space for teachers to target students' learning needs to increase student achievement. Often teacher candidates feel a disjuncture between theory and practice; however, to combat this dilemma, action research can easily be nested in the RtI model. The three tiers of RtI provide you a ripe opportunity to incorporate all five steps of the action research process. As described in chapter 1, the five steps in the action research process are issue identification, data collection, action planning, plan activation, and outcome assessment. The following section provides examples of how coursework can be used as a venue for action research within the three tiers of RtI.

## TYING ACTION RESEARCH TO COURSEWORK EMBEDDED IN RTI

At its core, RtI is a system intended to assess and meet the needs of all students by providing them with high quality instruction. It requires that you be in tune to each student so that you can identify and address learning issues early on, rather than waiting until the student falls further behind. In short, RtI is a process that should become a natural part of your practice. Because it requires you to examine your practice, identify issues, collect and analyze data, and make informed decisions based on those results, it is also a natural fit for action research.

In this section, we will illustrate how RtI aligns with a reflection-in-action mindset. We will describe assignments that we have used in courses for teacher candidates and outline how these could be launching pads for pursuing RtI as action research. The following table briefly describes how different coursework assignments are embedded within RtI. Further details are provided in table 8.1 about how each example targets each step of the action research project.

**Table 8.1. RtI and AR Summary Chart**

| | Tier I Assignment | Tier II Assignment | Tier III Assignment |
|---|---|---|---|
| Assignment Description | Using Mathematical Discussion | Strategy Implementation Project | Using Pen Pals Correspondence for Literacy Instruction |
| Step 1. Issue Identification | Providing high-quality, research-based instruction to all students in Tier 1. | Providing high-quality, research-based Tier II interventions to matched targeted students' needs. | Student has correctly written words with long vowel patterns. |
| Step 2. Data Collection | Collect observational and anecdotal notes on students' responses in mathematical discussions on daily instruction. | Identify students in need of intervention using current student data to analyze baseline performance. Write a brief description of the student(s) areas of strengths, weakness, and interests. | Collect pen pal letters, weekly spelling tests, and other pieces of student writing. |
| Step 3. Action Planning | Analyze students' responses to understand how students are thinking about the concept (understandings and misconceptions). Review mathematics research relevant to the content including common student misconceptions, the development of students' thinking, and effective representations and tasks. Discuss effective methods employed by other colleagues. | Determine an appropriate intervention by matching research-based interventions to the individual student's needs. In addition, an ongoing progress monitoring data plan is developed that indicates what type and how often data will be collected and analyzed. | Review literacy research about spelling instruction, word work, and writing instruction. Also, discuss this topic with colleagues in the field. |

| | | | |
|---|---|---|---|
| Step 4. Plan Activation | Plan next instructional episode based on students' learning needs as identified in Steps 2 and 3. Utilize knowledge learned from the research literature and through discussion with peers to make instructional decisions. | Teacher candidates should maintain a regular schedule of administration and scoring as progress monitoring is a vital part of the problem-solving process. In addition, interventions should be continued or adjusted according to student progress. | Plan to provide individual instruction on long vowel patterns and include independent practice through word sorting. |
| Step 5. Outcome Assessment | Collect observational and anecdotal notes on students' responses in mathematical discussions on daily instruction. Observe how Step 4 actions influenced students' learning. | Summarize project to determine the effectiveness of the current intervention plan. Evaluate and judge the effectiveness of the intervention. Determine whether to continue, revise, or discontinue the current intervention. Use graphing procedures is critical to this determination. | Review student data and observe how Step 4 influenced student learning. Also, reflect on how this experience influenced your instruction. |

## RTI AS ACTION RESEARCH IN TIER I: MATHEMATICAL
## DISCUSSIONS AS FORMATIVE ASSESSMENT

In mathematics methods courses for elementary teachers, we focus on developing teacher candidates' skills in eliciting and understanding students' thinking about mathematics; students are guided to use this information to inform their instruction. As part of this work, teacher candidates are required to plan and present a mathematics task and lead the students in a mathematical discussion based on the task (Chapin, O'Connor, & Anderson 2003).

To formulate a plan, the teacher candidate considers the major concepts of the task and then designs instruction to help students explore these ideas as they work on the task. Throughout, the teacher candidate considers questions and prompts that can help elicit students' thinking about the big ideas. The final instructional step in the lesson is a whole-class discussion about the students' solution strategies and their thinking about the big ideas of the task. The teacher candidate takes observational and anecdotal notes on the students' discussion.

As the teacher candidate analyzes the students' thinking, she identifies evidence of what individual students do and do not understand about the topic and considers how the instructional approach may have influenced these outcomes. Based on this information, the teacher candidate can make changes in her instruction to better meet students' needs. Used over time, this process may reveal patterns of difficulties among several students in the class or among specific students or groups.

Identifying patterns of need could be the basis for a targeted investigation into how to best address the students' difficulties. This is an example of how the action research mindset (action-data-reflection-action) is a natural fit with the RtI model, in the sense that it creates opportunities for you to examine, on a regular and continuous basis, your students' responses to your own instruction. You can consider whether the instructional methods used met the needs of all students in the context of the learning goals of the lesson and whether or not more specific, targeted action measures need to be investigated. In essence, this is action research. In the following sections, we will describe in detail how this approach aligns with the Five Step Action Research Process (see figure 1.2, chapter 1).

## RTI AS ACTION RESEARCH IN TIER I:
## SOLVING MATHEMATICAL PROBLEMS

### Step 1: Issue Identification: Identify an Area to Study

Tier I in RtI requires teachers to provide high-quality, research-based instruction to all students. Throughout, teachers must monitor students' progress to determine how they are responding to instruction. If a large number of students are not responding appropriately, this should be a signal that instructional adjustments should be made. If a small group of students are not responding, the teacher then must consider what additional supports may be needed to help individual students succeed.

One recommendation for instruction in RtI Tier I is the use of ongoing formative assessment. Formative assessment is defined here as assessment that is used to make decisions about instruction (William 2007). While many assessments may fit this description, what distinguishes them is the length of time between collecting information, analyzing it, and then responding to it (William 2007). The use of classroom discussion provides teachers the opportunity to use classroom talk to collect data on how individual students are responding to instruction, and then use that information to immediately adjust instruction to meet students' needs before waiting for the instructional methods to fail.

During the process, teachers may take anecdotal and observational notes on students' work on mathematical tasks, explanations of solution strategies, and responses to questions. These data can be organized in a chart so that students' progress can be examined over several episodes. Over time, patterns may emerge that indicate instruction is not meeting individual or groups of students' needs. For example, the teacher may notice that some students are having more difficulty than others solving mathematical problems. They are not able to understand what problems are asking, select appropriate strategies for solving, monitor their progress, or determine the reasonableness of solutions. As a result, the teacher decides to investigate the issue in an effort to help the students develop their problem-solving skills.

### Step 2: Data Collection

To further explore the problem, and determine if there is a real need for additional instructional support, the teacher will collect additional data on this group of students. In addition to the anecdotal and observational notes she is already collecting, she can collect the students' written work and explanations on selected problems. In addition, she can interview the students and ask them to orally describe and explain their strategies and thinking.

### Step 3: Action Planning

The teacher analyzes these data to understand how students think about and approach mathematical problems. The teacher looks for areas of strength in students' problem-solving skills, as well as areas of weakness. She then can review mathematics education research relevant to developing problem-solving skills. From this review, she learns about the effectiveness of instructional methods that focus on two areas: (1) metacognitive skills, or the ability to monitor and adjust one's own thinking, and (2) cooperative learning, which emphasizes the importance of participating in a community of mathematical learners (Thomas 2006).

The literature suggests that teachers can help students develop their metacognitive skills by serving as an external guide through using targeted questioning or providing students with a framework for their thinking. Studies have shown that such techniques have been effective, particularly when used within the context of learning specific mathematics content (Lesh & Zawojewski 2007; Thomas 2006).

## Step 4: Plan Activation

The teacher begins implementing the THINK framework (Thomas 2006) in her mathematics instruction. This framework is designed to help students monitor their thinking and guide their communication about their thinking while working on mathematical tasks. The teacher will use the strategy with the entire class. However, the teacher will use targeted questions to provide scaffolding for the students that have been identified. These questions may include: What is happening in this problem? Does it remind you of any other problem? What strategy do you think might work? How do you think it might help? How could you decide if your answer is correct?

In addition, the teacher, if necessary, will model her thinking about problems aloud. As she carries out her plan, the teacher is mindful of the students' backgrounds, prior experiences and knowledge, and other issues specific to the educational context, and she adjusts her activities accordingly. Figure 8.1 outlines the plan using a design worksheet.

## Step 5: Outcome Assessment

In this step, the teacher again collects data to determine the students' response to the instructional plan activated in step 4. She examines anecdotal and observational notes as well as students' written work and explanations on selected problems. In addition, she will re-interview the students and ask them to orally describe and explain their strategies and thinking. From these data, the teacher will determine how the actions taken in step 4, plan activation, are meeting the needs of her students. Based on what is learned, the teacher may continue with her instructional plan, while she continues to monitor students' response and makes modifications for specific students, as needed. If, however, some students are not showing desired progress, she may collect additional data and cycle through the process again.

| Additional Data Indicating Need for Intervention: | Instructional Procedures: | Times per week: __5__ Length of sessions: __60min.__ Tier I Initiation Date: ___ |
|---|---|---|
| • Observational and anecdotal notes on students' responses during discussions on mathematical tasks.<br>• Students' written work and explanations of their strategies.<br>• Interview transcripts of students' explanations of their mathematical thinking and strategies while solving problems. | • Implement the THINK framework (Thomas, 2006).<br>• For targeted students, ask additional questions to focus them on the steps of the framework.<br>• If needed, the teacher will model metacognitive skills by talking out loud about her thinking and process while solving a mathematical task. | **Progress Monitoring Plan:**<br>• Analyze observational and anecdotal notes on students' responses during discussions on mathematical tasks. (daily)<br>• Analyze students' written work and explanations of their strategies on mathematical tasks. (daily)<br>• Analyze interview transcripts of students' explanations and strategies while solving problems. (weekly) |
| **Person(s) Responsible for Data Analysis:** Classroom teacher | **Person(s) Responsible for Interventions:** Classroom teacher | **Goal Statement:** Improve students' skills in solving mathematical problems. |

**Figure 8.1.   Tier I Design Worksheet—Mathematical Discussions**

## RTI AS ACTION RESEARCH IN TIER II: STRATEGY IMPLEMENTATION PROJECT

During a special education methods course taken in conjunction with their elementary internship, teacher candidates complete a strategy implementation project. This action research project simulates the RtI process from start to finish by focusing on developing teacher candidates' knowledge and skills in making data-based decisions as they develop and implement an intervention to meet the needs of targeted students in need of remediation. Throughout this assignment the teacher candidates actively engage in action research by exploring essential components necessary to successfully work through the RtI problem-solving process. Below, we highlight the details of this assignment and how it aligns with the Five Step Action Research Process.

### Step 1: Issue Identification: Identify an Area to Study

The Strategy Implementation Project is designed to stimulate and lead preservice teachers through the steps of the RtI problem-solving process. For this assignment, prospective teachers are required to focus their efforts on the core academic areas of literacy and mathematics and collaborate with their mentor teachers. Since Tier II interventions occur in small groups, preservice teachers will be providing high-quality, research-based strategies to address the targeted needs of struggling students. In addition, it is critical that preservice teachers consider how they will regularly monitor students' progress to determine if the interventions are working.

### Step 2: Data Collection

Initial data collection revolves around using universal screening tools, benchmark assessments, diagnostic testing, and curriculum-based formative data to identify students and areas in need of intervention. Once a small group or an individual student has been identified, preservice teachers write a thorough description of the targeted students. This rich description includes a description of the areas of strengths, weaknesses, and interests that the student(s) exhibits, and a description of the academic area(s) that have been addressed for the project.

For example, one student developed her project around a group of kindergarten students who were at high risk for letter naming and initial letters sounds as indicated by classroom performance and Dynamic Indicators of Basic Early Literacy Skills (DIBELS) assessments.

### Step 3: Action Planning

After analyzing benchmark data, identifying students in need of intervention, and developing the description, preservice teachers and their mentors collaboratively construct a plan of action to meet these student needs. To complete this step, students use the Tier II design worksheet (see figure 8.2) to prepare a plan of action. Examples are included in italics on this figure that demonstrate how preservice students complete this critical step.

First, prospective teacher candidates list data that indicate a student is in need of an intervention in a particular area. Critical to this step is the development of a goal for the academic intervention. Next, prospective teachers and their mentors collaboratively research and determine when and what intervention(s) are necessary to change student performance for

**Additional Data Indicating Need for Intervention:/5**
- Universal screening results (*Samantha scored 6 on the DIBELS Initial Sound Fluency (ISF) measure. This suggests she is at some risk for future failure.*)
- Benchmark assessments (*As indicated on the kindergarten inventory Kristen's weaknesses include naming the days of the week, recognizing basic shapes, and recognizing letters. She identified only 4 of 26 uppercase letters and 0 of 26 lowercase letters.*)
- Observational and anecdotal notes (i.e., *James struggles to read with expression or with ease for him to understand the text he is reading. He is unable to decode unfamiliar text at a 2nd grade reading level.*)

**Instructional Procedures:**
- Research to determine appropriate intervention matched to student need (*Specifically designed instruction to promote independent reading skills using research based reading program such as Read Naturally*).
- Be specific. The more concrete the plan, the more likely the plan is implemented with fidelity and the more likely student(s) experiencing success. (*A range of strategies focused on tactile/kinesthetic experiences to increase her ability to recognize letters and initial sounds including Leapfrog phonics, alphabet recognition games, and leveled readers will be used.*)

**Times per week:** ___5___
**Length of sessions:** **Minimum of 30 min.**
**Tier II Initiation Date:** _____

**Progress Monitoring Plan:**
- Identify a measurement system for the intervention. (*At the end of each session, the student will graph their progress.*)
- Analyze progress daily using observational notes. (*Notes on what is proving to work or not work during each session will be taken. Intervention will changeaccordingly.*)
- Analyze progress monitoring probes as designed to monitor skills acquisition (*DIBELS ISF and ORF subtests assessment every two weeks*).

**Person(s) Responsible for Data Analysis:**
Classroom teacher

**Person(s) Responsible for Interventions:**
Classroom teacher

**Goal Statement:** Should include duration and be directly tied to area of student need.(*By xxx, James will increase his oral reading fluency score to 100 words per minute with 90% accuracy on a reading level 1.5 by December 2010*)

**Figure 8.2.   Tier II Design Worksheet– Strategy Implementation Project**

the targeted skills. Vital to this step is to determine the most appropriate intervention by matching research-based interventions to the individual student's or small group's needs.

The more specific and concrete the plan, the more likely the plan is implemented with fidelity and this increases the likelihood of the student(s) experiencing success. Third, a specific timeline for implementing the plan needs to be designed. This includes the frequency, time, and schedule for intervention sessions as well as developing a systemic progress-monitoring plan. This plan determines how often progress-monitoring data will be collected and analyzed throughout the intervention. Questions to assist and guide preservice students during this process include:

- Have you prioritized the needs of the student?
- Have you matched the intervention to be implemented with the specific needs of the student(s)? How?
- When setting goals have you considered the student's peer group (grade, class, subgroups, etc.) for comparison? Remember this is a required component of the RtI process.
- Have you scheduled progress-monitoring probes at least biweekly?
- How will you ensure the intervention plan is implemented with fidelity?
- How will your host teacher support you?
- When will you regularly collaborate with your host teacher to examine the data?

Once the worksheet is completed and approved by the mentor teacher and course instructor, students develop a brief narrative of the plan.

### Step 4: Plan Activation

Once the plan is developed and designed, prospective teachers should begin intervening as soon as possible. Throughout the semester, teacher candidates should maintain a regular schedule of administration and scoring as progress monitoring is a vital part of the RtI problem-solving process. By regularly scoring each measure and recording the results, teacher candidates are practicing data collection and analysis skills. Graphing templates are used to monitor student progress during the intervention plan period. The collection of valid and reliable data, as displayed in a graph form, allows the interns to determine how a student is responding to an intervention and, if needed, adjust the intervention accordingly. To provide assistance for preservice teachers, seminars targeting how to use Microsoft Excel to enter and graph data as well as make instructional decisions are offered throughout the semester (see figure 8.3 below).

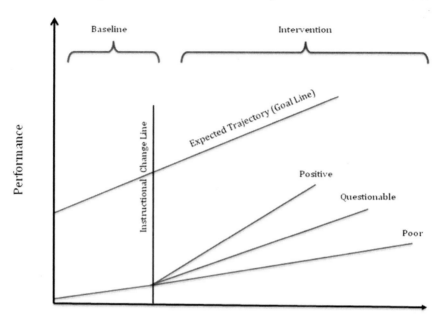

**Figure 8.3.  Example RtI Data Graph**

Last, questions to consider during the project are provided and include:

- Does the graph contain at least four (preferably six to eight) progress-monitoring points necessary to accurately create a trend line?
- Does the graph show the goal line (aim line) or appropriate benchmark? This should be correlated to your goal as outlined on your design worksheet.
- Does the data correlate with the goals of the intervention plan? In other words, is the graph monitoring the same need that was prioritized and addressed in the intervention plan?
- Is there data for each student? Is there a new graph for each intervention period if you changed interventions?

### Step 5: Outcome Assessment

The outcome assessment of the project is to summarize and analyze student-achievement progress based on intervention data to determine the effectiveness of the RtI intervention plan. Presenting data in a progress-monitoring graph is central to this part of the assessment as displayed in figure 8.3.

In addition, students share anecdotal notes from their research journal that can help explain inconsistencies in the intervention outcomes, including any inconsistencies in the data. Any changes or modifications of the intervention must also be discussed. Finally, recommendations for continued intervention and generalization necessary to assist the student in improving skill deficits are included. For instance, preservice teachers evaluate and judge the effectiveness of their plan, then decide to continue the current intervention, tweak or revise the intervention, discontinue the intervention and begin another, or refer students for further evaluation based on the outcomes of this project. Additional points students consider while writing this summary are:

- Has the intervention been implemented with fidelity (over sufficient time, consistently, and as designed)? Examine your Tier II design worksheet.
- Was the progress-monitoring plan appropriate? Explain.
- Is the data being reviewed valid? Explain.
- Has it been determined if the student response to the intervention was positive, questionable, poor? Explain.
- Based on this judgment, what are your future recommendations?

Using these guiding questions, as well as providing the examples of artifacts during the process, helps to showcase what is expected of our teacher candidates to complete this project.

## RTI AS ACTION RESEARCH IN TIER III: USING PEN PALS CORRESPONDENCE FOR LITERACY INSTRUCTION

This assignment matches teacher candidates up with a primary grade student as pen pals. The assignment provides the teacher candidate an opportunity to correspond with a primary grade student, which allows her to observe the student's written communication. This assignment demonstrates how action research aligns well with RtI's individual instruction focus found in Tier III. Each step of the action research project is briefly outlined in table 8.1.

Teacher candidates and primary grade students correspond three to five times throughout the semester. This provides the teacher candidate different pieces of student-written work to review and analyze through a teaching lens. The teacher candidate reviews each of the letters and writes three strengths and needs for each student letter that she receives. As the teacher candidate reviews the letters, she is asked to focus on phonics, spelling, writing conventions, and overall content. Once the teacher candidate reviews the three to five letters, she is required to write a reflection of what she noticed about the primary grade student's written communication, what she would plan for the student's instruction, and how she would implement this instruction. Teacher candidates should recognize how the RtI model creates a space for action research in all tiers; the pen pal assignment focuses on Tier III instruction.

As the teacher candidate corresponds with her primary grade student, she begins to better understand where the primary grade student's individual literacy strengths and needs lie. To think about this assignment as an action research project embedded in the RtI model, it is important to recognize that Tier III instruction focuses on individual student learning. This particular assignment lends itself well to action research in Tier III because each teacher candidate is already working with only one student.

## Step 1: Issue Identification

The first step in the action research process for the teacher candidate is to identify an area to study. In Tier III this is focused on one student's needs. The example provided for this assignment is based on the teacher candidate's recognition of the primary grade student's struggle with writing words with long vowel patterns correctly.

After reviewing the letters that she received from the primary grade student, the teacher candidate surmised that her pen pal understands that long vowel sounds are written differently then short vowel sounds; however, the primary grade student does not show mastery of written long vowel patterns. Reading and writing are reciprocal literacy skills (Flint 2008), thus justifying why this skill is an important action research topic for Tier III instruction.

## Step 2: Data Collection

Once the teacher candidate has identified an area of focus, data collection must be considered next. It is important to consider what types of data will provide the most information to you. In this assignment, the pen pal letters are what initially started the teacher candidate's inquiry. Now it is important to consider other pieces of data that will supplement this action research project.

The teacher candidate decided to also collect the primary grade student's weekly spelling tests and other writing assignments. These three pieces of data allow the teacher candidate opportunities to look across this student's work to see if (1) the misunderstandings when using long vowel patterns are consistent across different pieces of the student's work and (2) to systematically track how the student transfers the information learned throughout this action research project to different contexts.

## Step 3: Action Planning

This step is crucial to this action research. The teacher candidate who uses this assignment for action research in Tier III instruction needs to know the field of research on this topic and to understand her colleagues' perspectives on the topic.

Teacher candidates should collaborate with mentors at the school within which they are working for guidance about spelling, writing, and phonics instruction. Also, teacher candidates could engage in conversations with the professors at the university or college who teach the literacy methods courses. Both sets of colleagues will be able to provide resources for this topic. Other suggestions for finding literature in the field would be to search literacy journals such as *The Reading Teacher, Reading Research Quarterly, Literacy Research and Instruction,* and *Journal of Literacy Research.* These resources, along with collegial conversations, will help the teacher candidate better understand the primary grade student's needs in this literacy area.

Once the teacher candidate has completed steps 1–3 in the action research process, a design worksheet (figure 8.4) could be used as a framework for this project.

| Additional Data Indicating Need for Intervention: | Instructional Procedures: | Times per week: __5__ Length of sessions: **60min.** Tier III Initiation Date: _____ |
|---|---|---|
| • Student's written work such as pen pal letters, weekly spelling tests, other pieces of student writing | • Review literacy research on spelling instruction, word work, and writing instruction. • Discuss spelling/word work instruction with colleagues and collaborate • Provide individual instruction on long vowel patterns. • Provide time for independent practice through word sorting. | **Progress Monitoring Plan:** • Analyze pen pal correspondence (weekly) • Analyze spelling tests (weekly) • Analyze independent word sorts (daily) • Analyze other pieces of student writing (daily) |
| **Person(s) Responsible for Data Analysis:** Classroom teacher | **Person(s) Responsible for Interventions:** Classroom teacher | **Goal Statement:** Improve student's correct usage of long vowel patterns in written expression. |

**Figure 8.4. Tier III Design Worksheet—Using Pen Pals Correspondence for Literacy Instruction**

**Step 4: Plan Activation**

One instructional option for this step within this assignment would be to implement word sorting (Bear & Templeton 1998; Bear, Ivernizzi, Templeton, & Johnston 2008; Schlagal 2002) with this student. Word sorting allows students to see the relationships and patterns within our language (Bear & Templeton 1998; Bear, Ivernizzi, Templeton, & Johnston 2008; Schlagal 2002). Because this primary grade student struggles with long vowel patterns in her writing, it is important for the teacher candidate to help the student see connections between what she knows about the language and where she may be confused.

Through a word-sorting activity the teacher candidate can provide explicit instruction on long vowel patterns for the primary grade student. The primary grade student can then independently practice sorting the words into columns once the explicit instruction has been provided. This independent practice helps to support the primary grade student's learning. The teacher candidate is able to use the word sort activity for explicit instruction, independent practice, and assessment purposes for this individual student.

**Step 5: Outcome Assessment**

Action research is systematic and this is why this step is vital. Step 5 informs the teacher candidate of the student's learning throughout the process and provides a space for reflective practice. In this step the teacher candidate is able to analyze student data and any personal reflections that she made during the intervention about her teaching.

As you consider what instructional changes influenced the learning, you are engaging in reflective practice. This particular assignment allows the teacher candidate to focus on Tier III instruction that involves an individual student's reading and writing skills. Step 5 creates a space where the teacher candidate can look critically at the instruction and use data to understand how explicit instruction involving word sorting influenced this student's reading and writing skills. Further, through the varied pieces of collected, data the teacher candidate is able to conclude how her explicit instruction was transferred to different contexts over time (e.g., pen pal letters, weekly spelling tests, other writing assignments).

## ACTION RESEARCH AND RTI: FINAL THOUGHTS

RtI is clearly a natural fit with action research because it explicitly and systematically examines the needs of students, whether in groups or on an individual basis, with the action research reflection-in-action mindset. As you engage in action research within the RtI model, you will deepen your content knowledge and refine your instructional practice through a systematic inquiry stance. Action research within the RtI model creates a space for us to become more reflective and therefore more responsive to our students' needs; this exemplifies effective practice (Dozier, Johnston, & Rogers 2006).

RtI further supports the idea of action research being a mindset versus an add-on. As you shift your mindset about action research, more student needs will be met and student achievement will increase because you are responding to students' learning needs. Moreover, when you engage in action research that is nested in the RtI model and are able to explain and support the increase of student achievement through data, you have targeted the three areas of teaching knowledge (Cochran-Smith & Lytle 1999). This teaching knowledge deepens your understanding of the connections between theory and practice. Since we want teacher candidates to have a deep understanding of theory to practice connections, it is important for you to recognize how to engage in action research through the RtI model.

## QUESTIONS FOR REVIEW AND REFLECTION

1. How can action research focusing on RtI strengthen your knowledge of instruction?
2. How can action research focused on RtI influence your students' learning?
3. How can action research on RtI provide you with a better understanding of student learning?
4. How does action research on RtI help you provide responsive instruction?
5. How can you incorporate action research on RtI into a course assignment?

## REFERENCES

Bear, D. R., Ivernizzi, M., Templeton, S., & Johnston, F. (2008). *Words their way: Word study for phonics, vocabulary, and spelling instruction* (4th ed.). Upper Saddle River, NJ: Prentice-Hall.

Bear, D. R., & Templeton, S. (1998). Explorations in developmental spelling: Foundations for learning and teaching phonics, spelling, and vocabulary. *Reading Teacher, 52*(3), 222–42.

Bos, C., Mather, N., Dickson, S., Podhajski, B., & Chard, D. (2001). Perceptions and knowledge of preservice and inservice educators about early reading instruction. *Annals of Dyslexia, 51*, 97–120.

Bradley, R., Danielson, L., & Doolittle, J. (2007). Responsiveness to intervention: 1997 to 2007. *TEACHING Exceptional Children, 39*(5), 8–12.

Chapin, S. H., O'Connor, C., & Anderson, N. C. (2003). *Classroom discussions: Using math talk to help students learn, grades 1-6*. Sausalito, CA: Math Solutions.

Cochran-Smith, M., & Lytle, S. L. (1999). Relationships of knowledge and practice: Teacher learning in communities. *Review of Research in Education, 24,* 249–305.

Deno, S., Reschly, A., Lembke, E., Magnusson, D., Callender, S., Windram, H., Stachel, N. (2009). Developing a school-wide progress-monitoring system. *Psychology in the Schools, 46*(1), 44–55.

Deshler, D. D., Mellard, D. F., Tollefson, J. M., & Byrd, S. E. (2005). Research topics in responsiveness to intervention: Introduction to the special series. *Journal of Learning Disabilities, 38*(6), 483–84.

Dozier, C., Johnston, P., & Rogers, R. (2006). *Critical literacy, critical teaching: Tools for preparing responsive teachers*. New York: Teachers College Press.

Flint, A. S. (2008). *Literate lives: Teaching reading and writing in elementary classrooms*. Hoboken, NJ: John Wiley & Sons.

Fuchs, L. S., Fuchs, D., Compton, D. L., Bryant, J. D., Hamlett, C. L., & Seethaler, P. M. (2007). Mathematics screening and progress monitoring at first grade: Implications for response-to-intervention. *Exceptional Children, 73,* 311–30.

Fuchs, L. S., Compton, D. L., Fuchs, D., Paulsen, K., Bryant, J., & Hamlett, C. L. (2005). Responsiveness to intervention: Preventing and identifying mathematics disability. *TEACHING Exceptional Children, 37*(4), 60–63.

Fuchs, L. S., & Fuchs, D. (2007). A model for implementing responsiveness to intervention. *TEACHING Exceptional Children, 39*(5), 14–20.

Fuchs, D., & Fuchs, L. S. (2006). Introduction to response to intervention: What, why, and how valid is it? *Reading Research Quarterly, 41*(1), 93–99.

Fuchs, D., Fuchs, L. S., Compton, D. L., Bouton, B., Caffrey, E., & Hill, L. (2007). Dynamic assessment as responsiveness to intervention: A scripted protocol to identify young at-risk readers. *TEACHING Exceptional Children, 39*(5), 58–63.

Hale, J. B., Kaufman, A., Naglieri, J. A., & Kavale, K. A. (2006). Implementation of IDEA: Integrating response to intervention and cognitive assessment methods. *Psychology in the Schools, 43*(7), 753–70.

Hawkins, R., Kroeger, S., Musti-Rao, S., Barnett, D., & Ward, J. (2008). Preservice training in response to intervention: Learning by doing an interdisciplinary field experience. *Psychology in the Schools, 45*(8), 745–62.

Holdnack, J. A., & Weiss, L. G. (2006). IDEA 2004: Anticipated implications for clinical practice—integrating assessment and intervention. *Psychology in the Schools, 43*(8), 871–82.

Individuals with Disabilities Education Improvement Act of 2004, Pub. L. No. 108–446, 118 Stat. 37 (2004) (codified at 20 U.S.C.A. sec. 1400 et. Seq. [West 2003 & Supp. 2006]) (amending IDEA).

Jacobs, J., Gregory, A., Hoppey, D., & Yendol-Hoppey, D. (2009). Data literacy: Understanding teachers' data use in a context of accountability and response to intervention. *Action in Teacher Education, 31*(3), 41–55.

Kavale, K. A., Holdnack, J. A., & Mostert, M. P. (2006). Responsiveness to intervention and the identification of specific learning disability: A critique and alternative proposal. *Learning Disability Quarterly, 29*(2), 113–27.

Kovaleski, J. F., & Glew, M. C. (2006). Bringing instructional support teams to scale: Implications of the Pennsylvania experience. *Remedial and Special Education, 27*(1), 16–25.

Lesh, R., & Zawojewski, J. (2007). Problem solving and modeling. In Lester Jr., F. K. (Ed.). *Second handbook of research on mathematics teaching and learning* (pp. 1051–98). Charlotte, NC: Information Age.

Lose, M. (2007). A child's response to intervention requires a responsive teacher of reading. *Reading Teacher, 61*(3), 276–79.

Mastropieri, M., & Scruggs, T. (2005). Feasibility and consequences of response to intervention: Examination of the issues and scientific evidence as a model for the identification of individuals with learning disabilities. *Journal of Learning Disabilities, 38*(6), 525–31.

Mokhtari, K., Rosemary, C. A., & Edwards, P. A. (2007). Making instructional decisions based on data: What, how, and why. *Reading Teacher, 61*(4), 354–59.

Moore, J., & Whitfield, V. (2009). Building schoolwide capacity for preventing reading failure. *Reading Teacher, 62*(7), 622–24.

Murawski, W., & Hughes, C. (2009). Response to intervention, collaboration, and co-teaching: A logical combination for successful systemic change. *Preventing School Failure, 53*(4), 267–77.

No Child Left Behind Act of 2001. Pub. L. No. 107–110, 115 Stat. 1425 (2002).

Palenchar, L., & Boyer, L. (2008). Response to intervention: Implementation of a statewide system. *Rural Special Education Quarterly, 27*(4), 18–26.

Reschley, D. J. (2005). Learning disabilities identification: Primary intervention, secondary intervention, and then what? *Journal of Learning Disabilities, 38*(6), 510–15.

Roehrig, A. D., Duggar, S. W., Moats, L., Glover, M., & Mincey, B. (2008). When teachers work to use progress monitoring data to inform literacy instruction: Identifying potential supports and challenges. *Remedial and Special Education, 29*(6), 364–82.

Roehrig, A. D., Guidry, L. O., Bodur, Y., Guan, Q., Guo, Y., & Pop, M. (2008). Guided field observations: Variables related to preservice teachers' knowledge about effective primary reading instruction. *Literacy Research and Instruction, 47*(2), 76–98.

Schlagal, B. (2002). Classroom spelling instruction: History, research, and practice. *Reading Research and Instruction, 42*(1), 44–57.

Shen, J., & Cooley, V. (2008). Critical issues in using data for decision-making. *International Journal of Leadership in Education, 11*(3), 319–29.

Smith, R., & Leonard, P. (2005). Collaboration for inclusion: Practitioner perspectives. *Equity and Excellence in Education, 38*(4), 269–79.

Stecker, P. M., Fuchs, D., & Fuchs, L. S. (2008). Progress monitoring as essential practice within response to intervention. *Rural Special Education Quarterly, 27*(4), 10–17.

Thomas, K. R. (2006). Students THINK: A framework for improving problem solving. *Teaching Children Mathematics, 13*, 86–95.

William, D. (2007). Keeping learning on track: Classroom assessment and the regulation of learning. In Lester Jr., F. K. (Ed.). *Second handbook of research on mathematics teaching and learning* (pp. 1051–98). Charlotte, NC: Information Age.

Ysseldyke, J., Burns, M. K., Scholin, S. E., & Parker, D. C. (2010). Instructionally valid assessment within RTI. *Teaching Exceptional Children, 42*(4), 54–61.

# Index

# About the Contributors

## ELIZABETH K. BAKER

Elizabeth K. Baker's experience ranges from years of classroom to university teaching, as well as facilitating lesson study groups in public and private school settings. Lesson study has been integrated into her teaching methods course for science and mathematics teachers at Mills College since 2004. In addition to teaching, she currently is a researcher with the Mills College Lesson Study Group.

## JOHNNA BOLYARD

Johnna Bolyard is a former middle school mathematics teacher and district mathematics specialist. Currently, she is an Assistant Professor in the College of Human Resources and Education at West Virginia University. Her research interests focus on the development of mathematics teachers, particularly how K-8 teachers develop into mathematics teacher leaders.

## REAGAN CURTIS

Reagan Curtis, PhD, is currently Associate Professor of Educational Psychology, Program Evaluation, and Research Methods in the Department of Technology, Learning, and Culture at West Virginia University. Reagan teaches across the spectrum of research methodologies including statistics, program evaluation, action research, mixed methodologies, and qualitative research. His diverse research interests include the development of mathematical understanding infancy through elementary school, promotion of equity in STEM (Science, Technology, Engineering, and Mathematics) educational and career paths, and exploration of tools and pedagogical approaches to facilitate online instruction at the university level.

## DEBI GARTLAND

Debi Gartland, PhD, is Professor of Special Education at Towson University in Maryland. In addition to her interest in behavior management, she is involved in Professional Development Schools preparing dually-certified teacher candidates and in policy and advocacy for individuals with disabilities.

## MARK GIROD

Mark Girod is serving as Chair of Teacher Education at Western Oregon University. He holds a PhD in educational psychology from Michigan State University and specializes in science education and teacher development. His most recent work focuses on developing empirical connections between teacher preparation, teaching, and P–12 student learning.

## DAVID HOPPEY

David Hoppey is a former middle school special educator who received his PhD from the University of Florida. Currently, he is an assistant professor in the Department of Special Education at the University of South Florida. His interests include inclusive teacher education, response to intervention, school reform, and professional development.

## GERALDINE C. JENNY

Geraldine Jenny formerly taught elementary students at various grade levels in Indiana and Pennsylvania. She is the coauthor of five books on children's creativity and several journal articles on diverse areas of research interest. She is currently an Elementary/Early Childhood professor and Student Teacher Supervisor at Slippery Rock University of Pennsylvania.

## MARIE LEJEUNE

Marie LeJeune is a former high school language arts teacher and reading specialist whose research interest areas include adolescent literacy, children's and young adult literature, and teacher research. She received her PhD in literacy studies in 2007 from the University of Nevada, Las Vegas. She is currently an assistant professor in the Division of Teacher Education at Western Oregon University.

## CATHERINE C. LEWIS

Catherine Lewis conducts research on lesson study at Mills College in Oakland, California, where she is currently Principal Investigator on NSF- and IES-funded research projects on lesson study. She has conducted research in Japanese schools for thirty years and published numerous articles and two books, *Educating Hearts and Minds: Reflections on Japanese Preschool and Elementary Education* (1995) and of *Lesson Study: A Handbook of Teacher-Led Instructional Change* (2002). Video of U.S. and Japanese teachers engaging in lesson study and additional resources are available at www.lesson research.net.

## AIMEE MOREWOOD

Aimee Morewood taught special education in an urban school district before pursuing her PhD at the University of Pittsburgh. Currently, she teaches undergraduate and graduate level literacy courses at West Virginia University. Her research interests focus on literacy instruction within preservice teacher education programs and effective professional development for inservice teachers.

## SUSAN H. PILLETS

Susan Pillets began her career in education teaching fourth grade in Baltimore City Public Schools before moving to Baltimore County Public Schools in 1995 to teach kindergarten. Currently, she is an adjunct professor of education at Stevenson University and is a member of the Maryland Professional Development School Network.

## RICHARD SAGOR

Richard "Dick" Sagor, former director of the Educational Leadership Program at Lewis and Clark College in Portland, is the founding director of ISIE (pronounced "I see"), the Institute for the Study of Inquiry in Education. Dick has worked as a site visitor for the United States Department of Education's Blue Ribbon School Program, consulted with numerous State Departments of Education and independent school districts across North America, and has provided staff development workshops for international schools in Asia, South America, and Africa. Dick's focus is primarily on "Data and Standard-Based School Improvement," "Professional Learning Communities," "Collaborative Action Research," "Teacher Motivation," "Leadership Development," and "Teaching at-Risk Youth." Dick has written ten books on action research and school reform and has received numerous awards for his scholarship and service in this area.

## NEAL SHAMBAUGH

Neal Shambaugh is an associate professor and graduate program coordinator of Instructional Design and Technology at West Virginia University. His degrees in Management Science, Curriculum & Instruction, and Instructional Systems Design are from Virginia Tech. He is the author of two textbooks on instructional design. Since 1999, he has been a university liaison with a public elementary/middle school and has mentored action research with new and experienced teachers.

## TRACY SMILES

Tracy Smiles is on faculty at Western Oregon University where she coordinates the literacy program and teaches literacy courses in the undergraduate and graduate programs. Her scholarly interests include: English language arts/literacy education; children's and adolescent literature, teacher preparation and professional development in elementary/middle school education; teacher beliefs and knowledge; professional coursework in teacher education; and case methods with emphasis on teacher research.

## ROBERT SNYDER

Robert Snyder began his career in education as a fifth grade teacher at the North Penn School District in Pennsylvania, before moving on to teach sixth grade at the Moniteau School District, also in Pennsylvania. Dr. Snyder received a Bachelor of Science degree in Elementary Education in 1991, while simultaneously earning commission as an Officer in the United States Army Reserve from Slippery Rock University (SRU). Dr. Snyder has received many academic accolades, both military and civilian, and some of his highlights include the Pennsylvania Teacher Excellence Award and the SRU President's Award for Teaching Excellence. Dr. Snyder holds Master of Education degree in Elementary Science and Mathematics from SRU, a PhD in Instruction and Learning with an emphasis in Science Education from the University of Pittsburgh, and is presently a professor in the Elementary Education Department at SRU.

## LINDA TAYLOR

Linda Taylor holds an EdD from Ball State University. She has experience as a pre-k and kindergarten teacher, and is currently an assistant professor of Elementary Education.

## JACI WEBB-DEMPSEY

A former high school art teacher, Jaci Webb-Dempsey currently teaches at Fairmont State University where she coordinates the action research sequence for teacher candidates in the undergraduate and graduate programs and provides supportive professional development for university liaisons and PDS faculty. She has also worked with statewide efforts in West Virginia to promote principal leadership through school-based action research teams and with colleagues at West Virginia University to study the action research process.

## STEVE WOJCIKIEWICZ

Steve Wojcikiewicz graduated from the University of Notre Dame and got his start in teaching through the Alliance for Catholic Education service program. After spending three years teaching high school social studies and band, during which he earned his M.A.T. from the University of Portland, he moved on to a PhD program in educational psychology at Michigan State University, where he was supported by a University Distinguished Fellowship. In the midst of his graduate studies, he spent six seasons working as a deckhand, engineer, and officer aboard educational sailing vessels. He is currently an assistant professor of teacher education in the College of Education at Western Oregon University.

# About the Editor

**Dr. Robert P. Pelton** is currently a professor in the School of Education at Stevenson University, Stevenson, Maryland. Prior to working at the university level, Robert had an accomplished K–12 teaching career. He began teaching students with exceptional learning needs in an integrated K–third grade classroom, went on to teach middle and high school social studies, then returned to special education where he worked with middle school students categorized as having emotional and behavioral disorders. Through all these experiences, Dr. Pelton saw the value in using classroom-based data to shape his instructional methods.

Dr. Pelton has presented nationally and internationally on the topic of action research. Notably, he was invited as a panelist by the International Council on Education for Teaching (ICET) World Assembly in Hong Kong to address the topic of using action research in teacher preparation programs around the world. He is very active in professional development schools, where he assists teacher interns in using classroom data within the action research process to make instructional decisions. Dr. Pelton is also a consultant at Epiphanies Inc., where he effectively uses the action research model to help build and strengthen educational outreach programs.

CPSIA information can be obtained at www.ICGtesting.com
264283BV00002B/2/P